Fleet Street & Other Poems by John Davidson

John Davidson was born at Barrhead, East Renfrewshire on 11th April 1857.

In 1862 his family moved to Greenock and there he began his education at Highlanders' Academy. Davidson would now spend many years at school and the beginnings of a career in various industries before gaining employment in various schools.

By now literature was a large part of his activities and his first published work was 'Bruce, A Chronicle Play' in 1886. Four other plays quickly followed including the somewhat brilliant pantomimic 'Scaramouch in Naxos' (1889).

With his reputation gradually providing an income he was also able to explore his true medium; Verse. 'In a Music Hall and Other Poems' (1891) together with 'Fleet Street Eclogues' (1893) were ample proof that he possessed a quite rare, genuine and distinctive poetic gift.

Davidson now turned further and further towards verse. In 1894 he published his most popular volume, 'Ballads and Songs' (1894), and this was followed by a further 'Fleet Street Eclogues' (Second Series) (1896) and by 'New Ballads' (1897) and 'The Last Ballad' (1899).

As the new century dawned Davidson was hard at work on a series of 'Testaments', in which he gave definite expression to his philosophy and were published over a seven year period; 'The Testament of a Vivisector' (1901), 'The Testament of a Man Forbid' (1901), 'The Testament of an Empire Builder' (1902), and 'The Testament of John Davidson' (1908).

However, on 23rd March 1909, with his finances in ruins, the onset of cancer and profound hopelessness and clinical depression he left his house for the last time. His body was only found on September 18th by some local fishermen.

Index of Contents

PREFACE

The time has come to make an end. There are several natives. I find my pension is not enough; I have therefore still to turn aside and attempt things for which people will pay. My health also counts. Asthma and other annoyances I have tolerated for years; hut I cannot put up with cancer.

I thought this might be my last hook, and intended five poems, 'Cain', 'Judas'. 'Cæsar Borgia', 'Calvin', and 'Cromwell', under the general title, 'When God Meant God', to be the principal contents. 'Cain' is the only one of these poems which I have written. I should have concluded the volume with a second Testament in my own person, insisting that men should no longer degrade themselves under such appellations as Christian, Mohammedan, Agnostic, Monist, etc. Men are the Universe become conscious; the simplest man should consider himself too great to he called after any name.
J. D.

FLEET STREET

Wisps and rags of cloud in a withered sky,
A strip of pallid azure, at either end.
Above the Ludgate obelisk, above
The Temple griffin, widening with the width
Below, and parallel with the street that counts
Seven hundred paces of tesselated road
From Ludgate Circus west to Chancery Lane:
By concrete pavement flanked and precipice
Of windowed fronts on this side and on that,
A thoroughfare of everything that hastes.
The sullen tavern-loafers notwithstanding
And hawkers in the channel hunger-bit.

Interfluent night and day the tides of trade,
Labour and pleasure, law and crime, are sucked
From every urban quarter: through this strait
All business London pours. Amidst the boom

And thud of wheel and hoof the myriad feet
Are silent save to him who stands a while
And hearkens till his passive ear, attuned
To new discernment like an erudite
Musician's, which can follow note by note
The part of any player even in the din
And thrashing fury of the noisiest close
Orchestral, hears chromatic footsteps throb,
And tense susurrant speech of multitudes
That stride in pairs discussing ways and means.
Or reason with themselves, in single file
Advancing hardily on ruinous
Events; and should he listen long there comes
A second-hearing like the second-sight
Diviners knew, or as the runner gains
His second-breath; then phantom footsteps fall.
And muffled voices travel out of time:
Alsatians pass and Templars; stareabouts
For the new motion of Nineveh; morose
Or jolly tipplers of the Bolt-in-Tun,
The Devil Tavern; Johnson's heavy tread
And rolling laughter; Drayton trampling out
The thunder of Agincourt as up and down
He paces by St. Dunstan's; Chaucer, wroth,
Beating the friar that traduced the state;
And more remote, from centuries unknown,
Rumour of battle, noises of the swamp,
The gride of glacial rock, the rush of wings,
The roar of beasts that breathed a fiery air
Where fog envelops now electric light.
The music of the spheres, the humming speed
Centrifugal of molten planets loosed
From pregnant suns-to find their orbits out,
The whirling spindles of the nebulae.
The rapture of ethereal darkness strung
Illimitable in eternal space.

Fleet Street was once a silence in the ether.
The carbon, iron, copper, silicon,
Zinc, aluminium vapours, metalloids,
Constituents of the skeleton and shell
Of Fleet Street — of the woodwork, metalwork,
Brickwork, electric apparatus, drains
And printing-presses, conduits, pavement, road —
Were at the first unelemented space,
Imponderable tension in the dark
Consummate matter of eternity.
And so the flesh and blood of Fleet Street, nerve

And brain infusing life and soul, the men,
The women, woven, built and kneaded up
Of hydrogen, of azote, oxygen,
Of carbon, phosphorus, chlorine, sulphur, iron.
Of calcium, kalium, natrum, manganese,
The warm humanities that day and night
Inhabit and employ it and inspire.
Were in the ether mingled with it, there
Distinguished nothing from the road, the shops.
The drainpipes, sewage, sweepings of the street
Matter of infinite beauty and delight
Atoning offal, filth and all offence
With soul and intellect, with love and thought;
Matter whereof the furthest stars consist.
And every interstellar wilderness
From galaxy to galaxy, the thin
Imponderable ether, matter's ghost.
But matter still, substance demonstrable
Being the icy vehicle of light.

Flung off in teardrops spirally, or caste
In annular fission forth like Saturn's hoops.
Earth and the planets girdled solar space,
The offspring and the suburbs of the sun.
In rings or drops — the learned are unresolved
How planets and their satellites arrive;

But vision, vouching both, is more obsessed
By Saturn's way of circles here at hand.
Saturn has uttered many moons; his rings
May be the last abortive birth of powers
Luniparous unmatched in heaven; or else
These still-born undeveloped satellites
Denote an overweening confidence
Determined, risking all, on something new.
Having outstreated spirally and well
A brilliant series of customary moons,
The hazardous and genial orb began
A segregation annular instead,
Attempting boldly the impossible,
Thus to become the wonder of the skies
For ever hampered with the rings we see.
Stupendous error still eclipses net
Achievement; as in art the Sistine roof
Sublimely figured, or hardihood in war
That wastes a troop for glory, or as earth
In sheer terrestrial wantonness flung up
The Maripesan Vale, so in the skies

The most enchanting vision of the night,
Our belted Saturn shines, extravagance
Celestial jewelled with its dazzling fault.

Now, in the ether with all the universe.
And in the nebula of our solar scheme,
Fleet Street and Saturn's rings were interfused,
One mass of molecules being set apart
For the high theme of wonder and the butt
Of speculation, and the other doomed,
Although the most renowned throughout the world.
To be a little noisy London street.
How think we then? The metal, stone and lime,
Brick, asphalt, wood, the matter that renews
The shell of Fleet Street, does it still begrudge
The luminous zones with which it once was blent
Their lofty glory? Or must the carapace
Of Fleet Street, welded of the selfsame stuff
As man, be utterly oblivious? Thought
And passion, envy, joy — are these unfelt
By carbon, iron, azote, oxygen.
And other liberal substances that know
Rejoice and suffer in mankind, when power
Selective turns them into street? Things wrought
By us, are they, too, psychophysical?
Do these piled storeys and purlieus quaint of square
And alley envy Saturn's belts — a brief,
Not outwardly distinguished urban street
Upon a planet only remarkable
Among the spheres for insignificance.
And they so lovely and unparagoned
A thousand million of mundane miles away?
Are able editors, leader-writers, apt
Telegraphists and printers, the only soul
In Fleet Street, they, its only consciousness?
Perhaps the bricks remember. Who can tell
When filthy fog comes down and lights are out,
Machinery still, and traffic at the ebb.
If idle streets with time to meditate
Resent enforced passivity? I think
The admirable patience of the bricks
May fail them of a Sunday. Imagine it:
To be for ages unalterable brick,
Sans speech or motion, nameless in a wall
Among a million bricks alike unknown!
I think the splendid patience of the bricks
Gives out in darkness and foul weather, even
To the length of envying the wonderful

Exalted destiny of Saturn's belts;
And then I long to tell them, if I could,
How much more happy their condition is
Than that of rubbish revolving endlessly
In agonies of impotent remorse
About the planet it deserted. Thus
Should I exhort them: — Bricks, beloved bricks,
My brethren of the selfsame ether bred,
I hold it very beautiful of you
To think so handsomely of Saturn's rings,
Your old companions in the nebula;
But I can tell you and I'll make you know,
Your fate is not inferior to theirs.
These seeming jewelled zones that shine so bright
Are the mere wreck of matter, broken bits,
Detached and grinding beaches of barren rock
Hung up there as a menace and a sign;
Circular strips of chaos unredeemed,
Whirling in madness of oppugnant powers.
Whether his rings are Saturn's own attempt.
Abnormal and abortive, a brilliant ninth
Consummate moon to utter, or likelier still,
A leash of runaway material tides
That mutinously left their native orb
In molten youth to show all other stars
The real and only way to shine, and failed
Inevitably, being immature.
They are, beyond all doubt, unhappy zones,
Forlorp, remorseful, useless and ashamed.
Most beautiful, I grant you; beautiful
And useless, like all art: their fate it is
To be an agony of beauty, art
Inutile, unavailing, misconceived.
But you, most genial, intellectual bricks.
Most dutiful and most important, you
Are indispensable, an integral
Component of the world's most famous street.
Within your wholesome and convenient field
The truest miracle is daily done.
Never forget that men have tamed and taught
The lightning; clad it in a livery known
As news; and that without your constant aid
Our modern, actual magic, black and white.
Momentous mystery of telegraphy.
Resounding press, accomplished intellects
And pens expert would be impossible.
Take down the walls your myrmidons compose,
And Fleet Street, soul and body, ceases — fog

Unoccupied, wind, city sunshine sparse
And pallid claiming all the room that now.
Enclosed, accoutred, functioned, named and known,
Serves as the Dionysius' ear of the world.
Honour and excellence and praise are yours;
Be satisfied; be glad''.

But all the bricks,
O'erburdened and begrimed, in chorus sighed.
And as one brick, "Upon my cubical
Content, and by our common mother, I
Had rather shine, a shard of chaos, set
In Saturn's glistering rings, the exquisite
Enigma of the night, than be the unnamed,
Unthought-of copestone or foundation-stone
Of any merely world-distinguished street".

Applauding the ambition of the bricks,
I felt, I also, I would rather share
Dazzling perdition with material wreck
Suspended in majestic agony
About the withered loins of some undone
Wide-circling planet for the universe
To see, than live the dull life of a baked
Oblength of tempered clay, year in year out
Unnoticed in a murky mundane street;
But recollecting that the bricks were bricks
And not a planetary wonder, what
Event; soe'er awaits the world and time,
I reassured them: ''Gallant souls'', I cried,
"Noble and faithful bricks, be not dismayed I
I hear the shapeless fragments that make up
Æsthetic marvel in Saturn's girdles sigh
Disconsolately, as they chafe and grind
Each other, — Such an enviable fate
As that of any single solid brick
In Fleet Street, London, well and truly laid,
A moulded, tempered, necessary brick
In that most famous faubourg of the worlds
Exceeds our merits! Could we but attain
The crude integrity of commonplace
Cohesion even in the most exhausted, most
Decrepit, ruinous, forgotten orb
In some back alley of the Milky Way
How happy we should be! Remember, bricks,
Neither success nor failure envy spares;
Use envies art; art envies use. These moods
Will come; but regular bricks like you transcend

Them always. Be courageous; be yourselves,
Be proud of your telluric destiny".

With that the bricks took heart. "Why, so we are",
They said, "the ear of England! Let us be
Old England's ear!" And revolution beat
In smothered cries and muffled fusillades
Upon the trembling tympanal; empires
At war thridded the sounding labyrinth
With cannon; loyal peoples through the sea
And through the air by auditory nerves
Electric from the quarters of the earth
And from a hundred isles, their homage sent
With whispered news of aspirations, deeds.
Achievements to the Mother of Nations, she
Whose ever vigilant, clairaudient ear
Is Fleet Street.

SONG

Closes and courts and lanes,
Devious, clustered thick,
The thoroughfare, mains and drains,
People and mortar and brick.
Wood, metal, machinery, brains.
Pen and composing-stick;

Fleet Street, but exquisite flame
In the nebula once ere day and night
Began their travail, or earth became,
And all was passionate light.

Networks of wire overland,
Conduits under the sea,
Aerial message from strand to strand
By lightning that travels free,
Hither in haste to hand
Tidings of destiny:

These tingling nerves of the world's affairs
Deliver remorseless, rendering still
The fall of empires, the price of shares,
The record of good and ill.

Tidal the traffic goes
Citywards out of the town;

Townwards the evening ebb o'erflows
This highway of old renown,
When the fog-woven curtains close,
And the urban night comes down,

Where souls are spilt and intellects spent
O'er news vociferant near and far,
From Hesperus hard to the Orient,
From dawn to the evening star.

This is the royal refrain
That burdens the boom and the thud
Of omnibus, mobus, wain,
And the hoofs on the beaten mud,
From the Griffin at Chancery Lane
To the portal of old King Lud —

Fleet Street, diligent night and day,
Of news the mart and the burnished hearth,
Seven hundred paces of narrow way,
A notable bit of the earth.

THE CRYSTAL PALACE

Contraption, — that's the bizarre, proper slang.
Eclectic word, for this portentous toy.
The flying-machine, that gyrates stiffly, arms
A-kimbo, so to say, and baskets slung
From every elbow, skating in the air.
Irreverent, we; but Tartars from Thibet
May deem Sir Hiram the Grandest Lama, deem
His volatile machinery best, and most
Magnific, rotatory engine, meant
For penitence and prayer combined, whereby
Petitioner as well as orison
Are spun about in space: a solemn rite
Before the portal of that fane unique,
Victorian temple of commercialism,
Our very own eighth wonder of the world,
The Crystal Palace.

So sublime! Like some
Immense crustacean's gannoid skeleton,
Unearthed, and cleansed, and polished I Were it so
Our paleontological respect
Would shield it from derision; but when a shed,

Intended for a palace, looks as like
The fossil of a giant myriapod! . . .
'Twas Isabey — sarcastic wretch! — who told
A young aspirant, studying tandem art
And medicine, that he certainly was born
To be a surgeon: "When you try", he said,
To paint a boat you paint a tumour".

No
Idea of its purpose, and no word
Can make your glass and iron beautiful.
Colossal ugliness may fascinate
If something be expressed; and time adopts
Ungainliest stone and brick and ruins them
To beauty; but a building lacking life,
A house that must not mellow or decay? —
Tis nature's outcast. Moss and lichen? Stains
Of weather? From the first Nature said "No!
Shine there unblessed, a witness of my scorn!
I love the ashlar and the well-baked clay;
My seasons can adorn them sumptuously:
But you shall stand rebuked till men ashamed,
Abhor you, and destroy you and repent!"

But come: here's crowd; here's mob; a gala day!
The walks are black with people: no one hastes;
They all pursue their purpose business-like —
The polo-ground, the cycle-track; but most
Invade the palace glumly once again.
It is "again"; you feel it in the air —
Resigned habitués on every hand:
And yet agog; abandoned, yet concerned!
They can't tell why they come; they only know
They must shove through the holiday somehow.

In the main floor the fretful multitude
Circulates from the north nave to the south
Across the central transept — swish and tread
And murmur, like a seaboard's mingled sound.
About the sideshows eddies swirl and swing:
Distorting mirrors; waltzing-tops— wherein
Couples are wildly spun contrariwise
To your revolving platform; biographs,
Or rifle-ranges; panoramas; choose!
As stupid as it was last holiday?
They think so, — every whit! Outside, perhaps?
A spice of danger in the flying-machine?
A few who passed that whirligig, their hopes

On hjgher things, return disconsolate
To try the Tartar's volant oratory.
Others again, no more anticipant
Of any active business in their own
Diversion, joining stalwart folk who sought
At once the polo-ground, the cycle-track,
Accept the ineludible; while some
(Insidious anti-climax here) frequent
The water-entertainments— shallops, chutes
And rivers subterrene: — thus, passive, all,
Like savages bewitched, submit at last
To be the dupes of pleasure, sadly gay —
Victims, and not companions, of delight!

Not all! The garden-terrace hark, behold,
Music and dancing! People by themselves
Attempting happiness! A box of reeds —
Accordion, concertina, seraphine —
And practised fingers charm advertent feet!
The girls can dance, but, O their heavy-shod
Unwieldy swains I—No matter: — hatless heads,
With hair undone, eyes shut and cheeks aglow
On blissful shoulders lie: — such solemn youths
Sustaining ravished donahs! Round they swing.
In time or out, but unashamed and all
Enchanted with the glory of the world.
And look!— Among the laurels on the lawns
Torn coats and ragged skirts, starved faces flushed
With passion and with wonder! — hid away
Avowedly; but seen — and yet not seen!
None laugh; none point; none notice: multitude
Remembers and forgives; unwisest love
Is sacrosanct upon a holiday.
Out of the slums, into the open air
Let loose for once, their scant economies
Already spent, what was there left to do?
O sweetly, tenderly, devoutly think.
Shepherd and Shepherdess in Arcady!

A heavy shower; the Palace fills; begins
The business and the office of the day,
The eating and the drinking — only real
Enjoyment to be had, they tell you straight
Now that the shifty weather fails them too.
But what's the pother here, the blank dismay?
Money has lost its value at the bars:
Like tavern-tokens when the Boar's Head rang
With laughter and the Mermaid swam in wine,

Tickets are now the only currency.
Before the buffets, metal tables packed
As closely as mosaic, with peopled chairs
Cementing them, where damsels in and out
Attend with food, like disembodied things
That traverse rock as easily as air —
These are the havens, these the happy isles!
A dozen people fight for every seat—
Without a quarrel, unturbently: O,
A peaceable, a tame, a timorous crowd!
And yet relentless: this they know they need;
Here have they money's worth— some food, some drink;
And so alone, in couples, families, groups,
Consuming and consumed — for as they munch
Their victuals all their vitals ennui gnaws —
They sit and sit, and fain would sit it out
In tedious gormandize till firework-time.
But business beats them: those who sit must eat.
Tickets are purchased at besieged kiosks,
And when their value's spent — with such a grudge! —
They rise to buy again, and lose their seats;
For this is Mob, unhappy locust-swarm.
Instinctive, apathetic, ravenous.

Beyond a doubt a most unhappy crowd!
Some scores of thousands searching up and down
The north nave and the south nave hungrily
For space to sit and rest to eat and drink;
Or captives in a labyrinth, or herds
Imprisoned in a vast arena; here
A moment clustered; there entangled; now
In reaches sped and now in whirlpools spun
With noises like the wind and like the sea,
But silent vocally; they hate to speak:
Crowd; Mob; a blur of faces featureless,
Of forms inane; a stranded shoal of folk.

Astounding in the midst of this to meet
Voltaire, the man who worshipped first, who made
Indeed, the only god men reverence now,
Public Opinion. There he sits alert —
A cast of Houdon's smiling philosophe.
Old lion-fox, old tiger-ape — what names
They gave him! — better charactered by one
Who was his heir: "The amiable and gay".
So said the pessimist who called life sour
And drank it to the dregs. Enough: Voltaire —
About to speak: hands of a mummy clutch

The fauteuil's arms; he listens to the last
Before reply; one foot advanced; a new
Idea radiant in his wrinkled face.

Lunch in the grill-room for the well-to-do,
The spendthrifts and the connoisseurs of food —
Gourmet, gourmand, bezonian, epicure.
Reserved seats at the window? — Surely; you
And I must have the best place everywhere.
A deluge smudges out the landscape. Watch
The waiters since the scenery's not on view.
A harvest-day with them, our Switzers — knights
Of the napkin! How they balance loaded trays
And though they push each other spill no drop!
And how they glare at lazy lunchers, snatch
Unfinished plates sans "by your leave", and fling
The next dish down, before the dazzled lout
(The Switzer knows his man) has time to con
The menu, every tip precisely gaged,
Precisely earned, no service thrown away.
Sign of an extra douceur, reprimand
Is welcomed, and the valetudinous
Voluptuary served devoutly: he
With cauteries on his cranium; dyed moustache;
Teeth like a sea-wolfs, each a work of art
Numbered and valued singly; copper skin;
And nether eyelids pouched: — why he alone
Is worth a half-day's wage! Waiters for him
Are pensioners of indigestion, paid
As secret criminals disburse blackmail.
As Attic gluttons sacrificed a cock
To Æsculapius to propitiate
Hygeia — if the classic flourish serves!

"Grilled soles?" — for us: — Kidneys to follow. —
Now,
Your sole, sir; eat it with profound respect.
A little salt with one side scarce a pinch!
The other side with lemon; — tenderly!
Don't crush the starred bisection count the drops I
Those who begin with lemon miss the true
Aroma: quicken sense with salt, and then
The subtle, poignant, citric savour tunes
The delicate texture of the foam-white fish,
Evolving palatable harmony
That music might by happy chance express.
A crust of bread — (eat slowly: thirty chews,
Gladstonian rumination)— to change the key.

And now the wine— a well-decanted, choice
Chateau, bon per; a decade old; not more;
A velvet claret, piously unchilled.
A boiled potato with the kidney ... No!
Barbarian! Vandal! Sauce? 'Twould ruin all!
The kidney's the potato's sauce. Perpend:
You taste the esoteric attribute
In food; and know that all necessity
Is beauty's essence. Fill your glass: salute
The memory of the happy neolith
Who had the luck to hit on roast and boiled.
Finish the claret. — Now the rain has gone
The clouds are winnowed by the sighing south,
And hidden sunbeams through a silver woof
A warp of pallid bronze in secret ply.

Cigars and coffee in the billiard-room,
No soul here save the marker, eating chops;
The waiter and the damsel at the bar,
In listless talk. A most uncanny thing,
To enter suddenly a desolate cave
Upon the margent of the sounding Mob!
A hundred thousand people, class and mass.
In and about the palace, and not a pair
To play a hundred up! The billiard-room's
The smoking-room; and spacious too, like all
The apartments of the Palace: — why
Unused on holidays? The marker: aged;
Short, broad, but of a presence; reticent
And self-respecting; not at all the type: —
"O well", says he; "the business of the room
Fluctuates very little, year in, year out.
My customers are seasons mostly". One
On the instant enters: a curate, very much
At ease in Zion — and in Sydenham.
He tells two funny stories — not of the room;
And talks about the stage. "In London now".
He thinks, "the play's the thing. He undertakes
To entertain and not to preach: you see,
It's with the theatre and the music-hall,
Actor and artiste, the parson must compete.
Every bank-holiday and special day
The Crystal Palace sees him. Yes; he feels
His hand's upon the public pulse on such
Occasions". O, a sanguine clergyman!

Heard in the billiard-room the sound of Mob,
Occult and ominous, besets the mind:

Something gigantic, something terrible
Passes without; repasses; lingers; goes;
Returns and on the threshold pants in doubt
Whether to knock and enter, or burst the door
In hope of treasure and a living prey.
The vainest fantasy! Rejoin the crowd:
At once the sound depreciates. Up and down
The north nave and the south nave hastily
Some tens of thousands walk, silent and sad,
A most unhappy people, — Hereabout
Cellini's Perseus ought to be. Not that;
That's stucco— and Canova's: a stupid thing;
The face and posture of a governess —
A nursery governess who's had the nerve
To pick a dead mouse up. It used to stand
Beside the billiard-room, against the wall,
A cast of Benvenuto's masterpiece —
That came out lame, as he foretold, despite
His dinner dishes in the foundry flung.
They shift their sculpture here haphazard. — That?
King Francis — by Clesinger — on a horse.
Absurd; most mounted statues are, — And this?
Verrochio's Coleone. Not absurd:
Grotesque and strong, the battle-harlot rides
A stallion; fore and aft, his saddle, peaked
Like a mitre, grips him as in a vice.
In heavy armour mailed; his lifted helm
Reveals his dreadful look; his brows are drawn;
Four wrinkles deeply trench his muscular face;
His left arm half-extended, and the reins
Held carelessly, although the gesture's tense;
His right hand wields a sword invisible;
Remorseless pressure of his lips protrudes
His mouth; he would decapitate the world.

The light is artificial now; the place
Phantasmal like a beach in hell where souls
Are ground together by an unseen sea.
A dense throng in the central transept, wedged
So tightly they can neither clap nor stamp,
Shouting applause at something, goad themselves
In sheer despair to think it rather fine:
"We came here to enjoy ourselves. Bravo,
Then! Are we not?" Courageous folk beneath
The brows of Michael Angelo's Moses dance
A cakewalk in the dim Renascence Court.
Three people in the silent Reading-room
Regard us darkly as we enter: three

Come in with us, stare vacantly about,
Look from the window and withdraw at once.
A drama; a balloon; a -Beauty Show: —
People have seen them doubtless; but none of those
Deluded myriads walking up and down
The north nave and the south nave anxiously —
And aimlessly, so silent and so sad.

The day wears; twilight ends; the night comes down.
A ruddy targelike moon in a purple sky,
And the crowd waiting on the fireworks. Come:
Enough of Mob for one while. This way out —
Past Linacre and Chatham, the second Charles,
Venus and Victory — and Sir William Jones
In placid contemplation of a State!—
Down the long corridor to the district train.

RAILWAY STATIONS

I

LONDON BRIDGE

Much tolerance and genial strength of mind
Unbiassed witnesses who wish to find
This railway-station possible at all
Must cheerfully expend. Artistical
Ideas wither here: a magic power
Alone can pardon and in pity dower
With fictive charm a structure so immane.
How then may fancy, to begin with, feign
An origin for such a roundabout
Approach — so intricate, yet so without
Intention, and so spanned by tenebrous
And thundering viaducts? Grotesquely, thus: —
One night the disposition of the ward
Was shifted; for the streets with one accord,
Enfranchised by a landslip, danced the hay
And innocently jumbled up the way.
And so we enter. Here, without perhaps,
Except the automatic money-traps,
Inside the station, everything's so old,
So inconvenient, of such manifold
Perplexity, and, as a mole might see.
So strictly what a station shouldn't be.
That no idea minifies its crude

And yet elaborate ineptitude,
But some such fancied cataclysmal birth: —
Out of the nombles of the martyred earth
This old, unhappy terminus was hurled
Back from a day of small things when the world
At twenty miles an hour still stood aghast.
And thought the penny post mutation vast
As change itself. Before the Atlantic race
Developed turbined speed; before life's pace
Was set by automobilism; before
The furthest stars came thundering at the door
To claim close kindred with the sons of men;
Before the lettered keys outsped the pen;
Ere poverty was deemed the only crime
Or wireless news annihilated time,
Divulged now by an earthquake in the night,
This ancient terminus first saw the light.

A natural magic having gravely made
This desperate station possible, delayed
No longer by its character uncouth,
The innocent adventurer, seeking truth
Imaginative, if it may be, plays
His vision, penetrant as chemic rays,
Upon the delta wide of platforms, whence
Discharges into London's sea, immense
And turbulent, a brimming human flood,
A river inexhaustible of blood
That turns the wheels, and by a secret, old
As labour, changes heart-beats into gold
For those that toil not; all the gutters run,
Houses are daubed, with it; and moon and sun
Splashed as they spin. And yet this human tide,
As callous as the glaciers that glide
A foot a day, but as a torrent swift,
Sweeps unobservant save of time— for thrift
Or dread disposes clockwards every glance —
Right through a station which a seismic dance
Chimerical alone can harmonize
Even in imagination's friendly eyes.

Clearly a brimming tide of mind as well
As blood, whose ebb and flow is buy and sell,
Engulfed by London's storm and stress of trade
Before it reached the civic sea, and made
Oblivious, knowing nought terrestrial
Except that time is money, and money all.

Or when a portly dealer, well-to-do,
Chances to see it as he passes through,
Or boy or girl not yet entirely swamped
In ways and means and business of accompt,
About the many-platformed embouchure
And utterance of suburban life obscure
A liberal oeillade tosses, with a note
Chromatic, crimson van and crimson coat,
The parcel-post, and many a crimson shrine
Of merchandise mechanical combine
To reassure them as a point of war
Inspires the soldier; for the cannon's roar,
The trumpet's blast, the thunder of the drum
Are crimson motives; and the city's hum,
The noise of battle, and a ruddy sky
May echo in the selfsame harmony,
Save when the glance of age whose brisk affairs
Look up on 'Change, of youth untouched by care's
Inhibitory wand that palsies thought,
No other gracious sign appears, nor aught
Distinctly personal, innate or earned,
In the dull, rapid passage of concerned
Expression from the station to the street.
Until a dire resemblance of defeat
In one set visage hides the common face:
Such a premonstrant shadow of disgrace,
Such gray alarm, such sickening for despair
Is only seen in urban crowds, for there
The broken broker feels himself alone,
Exempt from scrutiny even of his own
Protean introspection, and as free
As genius, or as fallen spirit, to be
The very image of the thing he is —
A figure on the brink of the abyss,
The failure and the scapegoat of the mart,
The loser in the game, the tragic part
Wherein some novice mastered by the play
Without rehearsal triumphs every day.

II

LIVERPOOL STREET STATION

Through crystal roofs the sunlight fell,
And pencilled beams the gloss renewed
On iron rafters balanced well

On iron struts though dimly hued,
With smoke overlaid, with dust endued,
The walls and beams like beryl shone;
And dappled light the platforms strewed
With yellow foliage of the dawn
That withered by the porch of day's divan.

The fragrant, suave autumnal air
A dulcet Indian summer breathed,
Able to reach the inmost lair
Unclean of London's interwreathed
And labyrinthine railways, sheathed
In annual increments of soot;
Memories of regions parked and heathed.
Of orchards lit with golden fruit
Attuned October's subterranean lute.

But orchards lit with golden lamps,
Or purple moor, or nutbrown stream,
Or mountains where the morn encamps
Frequent no station-loafer's dream:
A breed of folk forlorn that seem
The heirs of disappointment, cast
By fate to be the preacher's theme,
To hunger daily and to fast,
And sink to helpless indigence at last.

From early morn they hang about
The bookstall, the refreshment-room;
They pause and think, as if in doubt
Which train to go by; now assume
A jaunty air, and now in gloom
They take the platform for a stage
And pace it, meditating doom —
Their own, the world's; in baffled rage
Condemning still the imperceptive age.

Like aromatic wine that does?
As wine will do with living clay.
The wonderful, anachronous,
Autumnal-summertidal day
Seduced a laboured soul to play
The idler: — (one who could rehearse
Unheard-of things; whose thoughts were gray
With travail, and whose reason scarce
Escaped the onslaught of the universe:

Yet one who waged an equal strife,

And, unsubdued, beyond the sad
Horizon of terrestrial life
In noisome cloud and thunder clad,
And death-cries of the past that bade
Repent, above the galaxy
Enthroned himself; and, sane or mad,
Magnanimously claimed to be
The soul and substance of eternity.)

He, then, to whom all things were great
By virtue of his native power,
Applauded autumn's sumptuous state,
And meant to share her golden hour —
Her kiss that moved the faded flower
To blush again, the haunting time
And witchcraft of her inmost bower,
Restoring for an afternoon
The bosom and the fragrant skirts of June.
He booked to Epping Street. The train
Drew out and clanking idly strayed
Along the line with dull refrain
That mocked the exigence of trade.
At Woodford milkmen long delayed
The journey; and at Snaresbrook noise
Broke out, and passengers inveighed
Against the line: such bitter joys
Two-faced occasion brings. At Theydon Bois,

At Chigwell Lane and Loughton, all
Complacent forest hamlets, folk.
Since chance itself might not forestall
Their sylvan leisure, tarrying, spoke
On footboards poised; and this one's joke.
And that one's parting comment, wound
A strand of laughter through the smoke
And pulsing steam, whose rhythmic sound
With pliant wheels a thundrous music ground.

From Epping Street where half a score
Inviting hostels lie between
The upper forest and the lower.
The bounds and metes of that demesne
That once from Waltham surged in green
Luxuriance to the northern tide,
The lover of the fall's serene
Miraculous renascence hied
By turnpike, woodland path and forest-ride.

A purple haze that scarce could keep
Diaphanous consistence spread
Above the ridged perspective deep
Of Epping Forest; overhead,
With arabesque shining thread
As manifold as jewelled dyes,
In varied beauty interwed
A snowy vapour damaskwise
Endued the tenderest of turquoise skies.

Ripples of cloud like silver strands
Escaloped by continual surge,
The seaboard of fantastic lands,
Defined the welkin's orient verge:
He heard afar the airy dirge
Of breaking billows, saw the foam
In heaven mantle, spindrift scourge
The zenith, and their shadows roam
Across the woods like coveys flying home.
A herd of clouds with fleeces rent
Flocked in the west; an aigret plumed
The low-hung northern firmament;
But in the south a shadow loomed
Like chaos out of eld exhumed
To re-engulf the world long lost
In time; and yet the darkness bloomed
With sprays of bronze like briars tossed,
With hidden flower and fruit of flame embossed.

He heard the woodman's fateful strokes
In Epping Thicket, blow on blow,
Where spaciously the loftiest oaks
In all the forest precincts grow.
The rose, the bramble and the sloe
Muffled the holly, hid the thorn;
And berries blushed with diverse glow
Of gradual colour like the morn,
Whose changing hues the ravished east adorn.

In many a dome of russet green,
Without a centre shaft to draw
The branches round it, might be seen.
Once more with tender-hearted awe,
The burning bush religion saw —
The nightshade's coral hanging free,
The scarlet hip, the crimson haw,
The swarthy bramble lovingly
Enwreathed as in a myriad-minded tree.

The bramble leaves, with iron mould
Distained, like metal foliage glanced;
The fluted beech, in ruddy gold
Accoutred bravely, countenanced
The yellow thorn whose hue enhanced
In turn the heather's rusty ore;
The bracken, faded all, advanced
Along the forest's pillared floor —
A tawny tide upon an emerald shore.

But eager frosts that braise and brand
Autumnal foliage still delayed;
Green was the forest, green the land,
A fibrous sward, a toothsome blade;
The cow-bells rang in every glade
Their quaint memorial refrain,
A ghostly sound by change unlaid;
The year stood still; and summer, fain
As in her prime, usurped the world again.
The chrysosperm in sunbeams pent
A largesse squandered. Rich as light
Of rainbow brede, the forest-scent;
And subtler, keener than the white
Aroma of the stars at night
That maddens lovers wandering late
Betrothed in destiny's despite;

As searching as the importunate
And supersenuous ether uncreate.

A doe stepped forth and pried about
With wondering look and watchful ear,
Then vanished. Venturous birds burst out
As in the heyday of the year
With summer song in snatches, clear
As water dropping in a well;
Harmonious from a turret near
Replied a silvery vesper-bell;
The braided light grew golden; evening fell.

In Highbeach Holt, a place alone,
A wonder of the world, antique
Protected beeches straightly grown,
Or pollarded of yore and meek
Transmuters of the shapeless freak
The iron wrought throughout the years
To symmetry, that all things seek

For ever, they, the verderer's
Most cherished vert in all his marks and meres,

Upon a forest fabric stood
Three-piles of leaves and fruitful mast,
That carpeted the upland wood
And crypts and bowery obscure and vast
In the close twilight waning fast:
Some scumbled moss, with here and there
A stroke of scanty herbage, cast
A chord of green, remarked and rare
Among the russet spreading everywhere.

All still and stately ancient trees,
With stem erect and ample bole.
Maintained their native majesties
In leafy robe and verdant stole
Invested, green from fork to poll;
Old, gnarled and thundersmitten, some
Uncouthly grew, the sylvan soul
By brutal accident become
A tortured wraith in hideous anguish dumb.

The saplings flourished straight and tall
Like living palisades a-row,
Their lance-like stems in vertical
And rhythmic parallels below;
Above like crayon lines that flow
Obliquely through each other, swart
Immingled boughs in writhen throe
A cross-hatched canopy athwart
The precinct flung and roofed the arboured cour

A silence like the deadened night
The ebon-pillared emerald walls
Immured; a dusky latticed light
Fulfilled the high-groined cloisters, halls,
Occult recesses, wildwood stalls
In glimmering chancel-aisles arrayed;
And violet beams at intervals
Illumed the forest-girdled glade
Through rents and loopholes in the beechen shad

With hue and form so diverse stored.
Beauty and wonder, vaulted space
By fantasy alone explored.
The solitude and rich embrace
Soul-clasping of that silent place

So sphered his vision, steeped his brain
In dreams, that he beheld no trace
Of mundane things, nor hint nor stain
Of twilight or of night, until again

He reached the city. Then and there
A potent urban spell subdued
The forest's, for the sorcerer
Of sorcerers is multitude.
Three railway-sirens closely brood
Together by the Bishop's Gate,
That ancient, famous neighbourhood;
And nowhere more profoundly, late
Or early, can the nameless sense of fate

In numbers immanent be felt
Than in these eastern haunts at night.
Where eddying tumults surge and melt,
Like clouds beneath remorseless light
In streets and garnished windows, bright
As for some celebration high,
While tides of transit at the height
In rival modes of passage vie,
And wheel and hoof and automobile ply,

Barbaric shouts and shrieks he heard,
Like cries of wrath or cries of ruth;
But no one laughed or spoke a word;
Master and man, and age and youth
In purposeless, intense, uncouth
Commotion seemed for ever lost.
Save those that wooed in saddest sooth
A hope forlorn, in all things crossed.
And yet resolved w live at any cost.

The gutter-merchants. At the kerb
Fifty and five, a ghastly row,
With faces hell could not perturb
So rigid were they in their woe,
Self-centred stood. Life's undertow
Had dragged them down; a few were old,
A few were young, though fallen so low;
But most were in their prime: they sold
Unnecessary trifles manifold.

A while he watched them wonderstruck;
And scornfully they watched again.
Not these the undistinguished ruck

And ordinary run of men!
Their mystery seemed beyond his ken:
What brought such mortals there, so strong,
So resolute? How, where and when
Had fortune thrust them forth among
The sufferers unsalvable of wrong?

Their eyes on fire, their wrinkles changed
To shadowed sculpture in the brute
Effulgence of the windows, ranged
Together closely, foot by foot.
Like giant marionettes, as mute,
As quick and as mechanical.
Fronting the shops, they made their suit
By signs alone; and each and all
Unhuman seemed, austere, asexual.

And yet in faces drawn and starved
The tale of many a lingering fight
With circumstance was deeply carved;
Of hazardous attempts to smite
A passage through the solid night
The outcast beats his head against;
To enter, maugre might and right,
A huckstering world, alike incensed
By challengers and suppliants, and fenced

About with adamantine hearts.
He thought, As well would it behove
The morning to invade the marts;
Or that the dawn should live and move
Within an iceberg! Nought can prove
More terrible than toil for hire,
Or toil at all, to these; the groove,
The settled habit men desire —
They find it torture and the nether fire.

"On every lip, on every brow
I see their dreadful secret lurk;
All work to them is thraldom now;
They hate to work, they cannot work.
This last expedient still they shirk,
And every day resolve to fly
From hell: — No hope, no fear, no quirk
Of conscience, in the public eye
Shall stand us there again who dare to die!

"But all have made it up with fate

Sincerely by the evening! Soon,
Or when the irksome night is late
And in the west the wintry moon
Disdains the city, or at noon
When the huge welter of the day
Goes thundering past them to a tune
They cannot sing, the old dismay
Victorious seems and death the only way.

"Diurnally recurrent strife!
Some carry poison; always there
The silent river flows; now life,
Now death, the makeweight of despair
Determines; but the end is ne'er
In doubt: — In utter obloquy,
In utter woe, we greatly dare
To live, since those alone are free
Who keep the power to he or not to be.

"Such is their dread, their awful lot —
To live with palsied souls and numb
Affections! Higher courage not
With sound of prayer or sound of drum
In battle or in martyrdom
Was ever shown by saint or knight!
They stand at gaze through wearisome
Eternities, by ruthless light
Betrayed and scorned and shuddered at, invite

"The passers-by to spend the pence
That keep them tortured in the pit
Wherein their supersubtle sense
Entrapped them, and the fire their wit
Prepared, their pride and passion lit!
Only the miracle, mankind.
Can face this hell of the unfit —
Only the universe enshrined
In lordly flesh and blood and lordly mind".

IN THE CITY

Is it heaven and its city-porch,
Or a ceiling high-hung of old
With lacquer fumed and scrolled
Of many a festal torch?

High heaven it is, and the day
With its London doom of smoke
No storm can quite revoke,
No deluge wash away.

When their march and song grow mute
In the city's labyrinth trapped,
The storms themselves are wrapped
In draggled shrouds of soot.

Whirlwinds by lightnings paced
To run their wild career.
With ragged gossamere
Of fine-spun carbon-laced,

As soon as they quit the shires
Are lost beyond all hail:
The mightiest tempests quail
In the midst of a million fires.

But the heavens are clear to-day,
Though their London doom of smoke
No storm can quite revoke,
No deluge wash away.

CAIN

My sons and daughters; children's children; Cain's
Posterity; — God, what a multitude
From one man's seed — hiding the sun!
They stop the air, and make this cave a tomb
Already! . . . What? I bade them? If I did,
'Twas not to stifle me. Stand from the door!
Let in the light, let in the breath, of heaven!

Now I remember why I bade them come.
Carry me out among them. All the air
That mantles earth invisibly, and fills
The bosom of the world, would scarce suffice
To word with power the thing I have to tell.

My sight grows keen again: I see them, — these
The offspring of my loins: — Enoch and Irad,
Sons and companions; generations; boys
That promise to be great — Jabal and Jubal,
And my namesake, Tubalcain. My lusty men,

My breeding women and my little ones,
My maidens beautiful, my young men chaste.
My blessing and God's curse be with you all.
Lie down about me, stretched at length; behind
There, sit or kneel; and let the standers ring
Us closely round, that every one may hear.

My children, I am dying. Very old
Am I. A thousand storms have shaken all
My members; and the moments, like a rain
That never lessens, falling day and night
Throughout the steadfast centuries have cleansed
My memory of the chances that befell: —
Our sojourns and our warfare and our work.
Our triumphs, travels, happinesses, pains,
My own especial charge and vigilance
For us and ours, as well as intimate
Affection, privy thoughts and single life.
From my remembrance like a landslip fall,
Leaving the naked rock of that event
Whereon our fate is founded. Many times
I thought to tell you, many times put off.
It may be said when I have made it known —
Often I told myself so: — Had lie kept
His secret to himself, our folk, unswayed
By knowledge, might have overborne divine
Intention, and the tribal fate decreed.
But I say. No. I fought God's will, and built
A city east of Eden. Void it stands, —
It, and the city, Enoch, which I named
After my eldest born, — silent and void
Except for beasts and birds: — you would not live
In houses, rooted, impotent as trees.
Why had God loosed you from the cumbering earth
And given you pliant limbs if not to roam
From place to place? Caves in the wilderness,
And in the desert camps, for sons of mine!
God had ordained it; deftly given us limbs
That He might curse us did we grow like trees
Where had His fugitives and wanderers been?
God cannot be escaped: He means that I
Should tell you. Fables, whispered closely, hum
About the watch-fires; and a lie believed
May sow a tribal fate more terrible
Than errantry like ours. This too, I know,
My children, — that I dare not, cannot, die
Until I tell you and I wish to die,
Being forwearied of the world and time,

I had a brother, Abel, whom I loved
As no man shall be loved by man again.
Companions were we when the world was young,
And only us of our nativity
To love the other for the other's sake:
Our gentle mates were second in our hearts.
Younger than I, he was the hardier;
And I in everything gave way, well pleased
That he should still excel, — and with his pride
In excellence well pleased. Our thoughts of God
Alone divided us, as such thoughts will —
Father from son, kindred from kindred, folk
From folk, until the world or God shall cease.

I dug and planted; studied nature's way;
And out of meagre grasses fostered grain,
Enhanced the zest, augmented and refined
The substances of fruits and roots and herbs.
My brother idled, angry in the sun
And sullen in the shade. At times he gazed
On Eden half a day in ecstasy;
Or dark with sin hereditary, wrath
And sorrow intermingled, frowned on heaven
Until he fell down pulseless, breathless, dead
It seemed, by fighting passions hacked and slain.
In rarer moods he wrought with me, perturbed
By mystery of the blossoms that unveiled
Such tender beauty, and with fragrance bore
The seed the earth enwombed: it maddened him
To watch how nature did, to know the thing
Achieved and not to understand: — "Shall folk,
The human fruit of blossoms that unite.
Be in the earth enwombed and live again?"

Not as the plants are we I answered still
His obdurate demand. "Released from earth,
Our birth, our growth, our life are in the air,
Though when we die the soil reclaims us: God
Appointed it. But in our seed we live
As blossoms do: — an all-atoning truth
That only tortured him. He knew no ease
In life, no respite found from doubt and dread
Except in force expended, powers employed.
Loving the heats and dangers of the chase,
Deep-bosomed, swift of foot, he overtook
The leopard flying for life; the lion feared
To meet him; from their bloody dens he dragged

The fiercest beasts and killed them weaponless.

At dawn upon an altar built of turf
And grafted in the earth, I daily spread
For God a grateful table, fruit and corn
In season. But my brother worshipped not
With me:— "I serve the Lord by killing things",
He told me when I asked him how he praised
The maker of the world, God's will it is",
He said, "that all His creatures should destroy
Each other: hoofed-and-horned devour the herb
Fattening themselves for fanged-and-clawed; the night
Devours the day; the day, the night; I kill
All things that are — beasts, fishes, birds, grain, fruit;
Darkness itself with fire I can dismember,
God's will is light and darkness, life and death:
Two utmost joys, to kill and to beget,
I share with God, creator and destroyer".

"But God is love", I said. "Seek not for God
In bloodshed. In the rapture of desire,
In busy peace of heart by day, in dreams
By night that sweeten sleep with paradise
Discover God".

"No; God is strength", he said.
"Hunger and carnage, lust and strife are God
Inspiring all His creatures, strong or weak,
In their divine degree".

"Save man!" I cried.
"Although with skins of slaughtered beasts we veil
Our nakedness, against the weather pitch
Pavilions in the desert, we devour
No flesh, nor stain our lips with blood; the earth's
Benignant bosom feeds us tenderly".

"Like sheep and kine-big-bellied things, the prey
Of lean ferocity! Since we can kill"...
He looked at me askance, a splintered fire
Burst from his eyes athwart the dawning thought:
Unwonted laughter shimmered in his face,
Like heat that vibrates from the sun-soaked earth
And makes a presence of the throbbing air.
"Since we can kill?" I echoed, knowing well
His dreadful meaning. "What you dare not speak
You will not do!"

"The thoughts that teem with deeds
Fulfil themselves unspoken. God delights
To rend and tear, to lap the smoking blood.
God's a voracious God; the uddered things
And haunched, the sagging entrails are His prey
Assigned; the tiger and the lion. His fangs.
His appetite and maw. Were we to dip
Our mouths in blood, like those beloved beasts.
It would rejoice the hungry heart of God.
And for our own behoof, — if flesh of fruit.
The blood of berries, mellow sap of pulse
And marrow of the grain can nourish strength
Like ours, what keener zest, what ampler might
A more compact, a more essential fare
Might goad our palates with and prime our nerves!
The loins of timid things that chew the cud
Mature the pasturage we cannot eat
For our superior nurture. I shall flesh
My appetite — God's appetite in me".
"Not God's!" I cried in wrath. "The God of man,
Lions and tigers in his similitude
Would never frame".

"In whose resemblance, then?
Brother, God shaped His wanton, ravening beasts
In likeness of His cruelty— the mark,
The very soul and character of God.
So sure am I that God designed His men
To feed on flesh and blood as lions do
That I shall challenge it. You offer God
The sweetness and the ripeness of the earth
Upon your turfen table, and salute
The dawn. To-morrow at your side
I shall upon an altar built of stone —
The monument of what must there befall—
A living victim sacrifice, while both
Entreat a sign from heaven, nor cease to pray
Until God's will and pleasure are made known.
How say you? Dare you put God to the test?"

"In His great name!" I cried, assured that now
The man I loved would know the heart of God,
So human, so divine — as I believed.
Wet with the vapour that involved the earth,
A sheaf of corn across my shoulders slung,
With apples in a basket in my right.
And in my other hand a bunch of grapes,
I climbed the hill before the dawn, and laid

My offering on my altar, sure of heaven.
My brother followed, leading in a withe,
A white bull, whiter than the rolling fog
That wreathed its horns. He spoke not; nor did I.
But when the touch of morning lit the crests
Of Havilah o'erhanging Eden, doubt
Assailed me suddenly. I crushed the grapes
In eager hands, staining the golden corn.
The ruddy fruit — a rite then first observed
Unwittingly, for all my being shook
With abject fear of God, unknown before,
But soon about to overcast the world —
Though not on us the woeful shadow lies:
Accursed of God we earnestly disclaim
The cowardice that hallows vengeful wrath
And terror of the inconceivable.
It was in ignorance I crushed the grapes.
Inspired by God against my conscious will
To pour out blood before Him. Yet I spoke
My prayer— our prayer: — together children, pray
Once more with me— with Cain before he dies: —
"O God of men, we thank Thee for the earth,
For life and death, for labour and for rest,
For day and night, for seasons, times and tides;
Empower our souls with faith; direct our steps
I In ways of pleasantness and paths of peace;
And thine shall be the. praise for ever more.
Creator of the world, the just, the true,
The merciful, the gracious God of men".

I made my invocation, unaware
How insolent it was; and on my knees
Implored a token of acceptance. Through
The valley rolled the mist; a pearly smoke
O'ercanopied the guarded bowers, and depths
Profound of sylvan shadow, that the day,
Unveiling, deepened; sundered mountain-tops,
Pellucid in the crimson gorge of dawn.
Above the earth like pendent meteors burned;
The Pishon wound among the woods below,
The mirror of the morning streaming blood.
With amber and with beryl-stone enchased.
But God was silent and allowed no sign.
Then as the sun surmounted Havilah,
My brother, kneeling strongly on the bull's
Ascendant shoulder, bore the creature down:
His left hand gripped its underjaw, and bent
Its tossing head backward and stretched its throat;

His right implanted in its curded neck
The ivory blade, that out he drew again
Ensanguined all its length, swiftly and smooth
As though the spouting blood had thrust it forth.
His grip upon its muzzle chokdd the bull's
Affrighted roar, his puissance overcame
Its agony, and held it till it died,
Upon the dripping altar offered up,
Its milk-white dewlap and its milk-white flank
With bloody foliage strown and flowers of death.

Mastering his bosom as a rough-wrought sea
Recovers tidal measure when the storm
Desists, my brother tarried, vigilant
To repossess himself; then stepping slow
With majesty and grace unseen on earth
Before that morn of world-transforming chance,
He left the altar, and flung his looks aloft
Where sumptuously the vintage of the east
Empurpled all the peaks of Havilah,
And westward where belated orbs of night,
So limpid was the heaven-spanned firmament,
Between Assyrian summits darkling swung
Their crystal lamps. The beauty of the world
Rebuked him for a moment—or I thought
It did; the pause, the doubt, if doubt or pause
Began, was seen by me, not felt by him,
And died upon its birth.

"Almighty God",
With hardihood devout he said, "accept
This blood that steams new-spilt, and this. Thy brute,
New-slain to please Thee; and bestow a sign
Of Thy acceptance that Thy men may know
How strenuous, how absolute Thou art,
A God alive, an active God, a God
Delighting in a bloody sacrifice.
As Thy ferocious creatures take delight
In slaughter and the flesh of rams and bulls

Forthwith while yet the coil of breath, that bore
His supplicative arrogance, aspired
Unseen in the unseen, the cloudless top
And tented blue of heaven, disparting, showed
As in a fruit that bursts, the sanguine seed
And crimson heart of glory, lucid shapes
Celestial and pavilions thronged with life, —
A transient revelation, but beheld

In vision still, as obvious as the sun,
By my surviving eyes that wait on death.
Heaven opened and heaven closed: adown the gulf
Unmeasured and aerial steep of space
A saffron flame, in figure like a frond
The wind inwraps and tapers skywards, fell
Directly on my brother's altar, lapped
The hissing blood as with a hundred tongues.
And, fawning o'er the carcase, burnt it up.
Transfigured by acceptance of the blood
He spilt, my brother laughed aloud, and called
Exultantly on God, "Divine destroyer,
Reveller in life and death, let me partake
With Thee!" he cried. Dropping the ivory blade
That broached the creature's life, before the fire
Had licked the flesh from all the blackened ribs,
He grasped a smouldering handful and scorched his mouth
With God's accepted sacrifice. Appalled
To see a man, my brother, taste the food
Of savage brutes, my senses failed, my heart
Stood still a space; then thundering in my ears
A tide of passion swept me from myself,
A thousand judgments like a gathered storm
Burst in my mind:— "If God", I thought and seized
My brother's blade, "delights in blood of beasts.
The blood of men should fill the cup divine
With happiness ineffable Straightway
I flung an arm about my brother's neck,
And drove the bloodstained ivory through his heart.
He fell without a murmur: the breath of life
Escaped his grinding teeth, his parted lips;
The wonder in his eyes dismays me still, —
And overwhelmed then. But when I looked
To see the vaulted base of paradise
Re-open, and a sheaf of fire descend,
No fissure, chink or crevice, broke the blue
Immensity that hid the infinite.

Thus God refused my brother's blood — the man
I loved, and killed that he might live divine
Eternally, a part of God; for that,
Within the madness of the murder, sang
Like music in a tempest. God preferred
A bull's blood to my brother's: — still I think,
Old, dying as I am, something went wrong
In heaven. Howbeit when I saw him dead
And unaccepted, not the saltest tear
Assuaged the fiery horror of myself

That melted all my strength: in thunder drops
The sweat splashed from my brow; a core of pain
Without remission rising in my gorge,
Hot, hard and noisome sickened me; I beat
My breast; I fell; I rose; I fled, and plunged
In wooded darkness where the thicket wove
A thorny canopy. My fate, my doom! —
God had me there alone, unhelped by light,
By power and beauty of the widespread world.
Immediately the still and awful voice.
Whose accents are omnipotence, besieged
My soul and said, "Thy brother, where is he?"
I answered, as men answer God, at once,
I know not, I. Am I my brother's keeper?''

"What hast thou done?" God said. "Thy brother's blood.
That crieth from the ground, hath cursed the ground
For thee. When thou shalt till the ground that oped
Her mouth to drink thy brother's blood, poured by thy hand,
Henceforth it shall not yield thee of her strength.
A fugitive and a wanderer shalt thou be
Upon the earth!"

I answered in the rapt
Despair the presence and the ire of God
Begat, "I know that my iniquity
Can never be forgiven. Behold, since Thou
Hast reft from me the favour of the ground
And turned Thy countenance away, and I
Shall be a wanderer, it shall come to pass
That whosoever findeth me shall slay me
"Therefore", said God, "whoever slayeth Cain
On him a sevenfold vengeance shall be taken''.

With that God set His mark upon my brow.
Which none behold unawed or look on twice.

I have told the truth; no more remains to tell:
God's curse is on us; and we make it do.
Our errant life is not unhappy; fear,
That harrows others, is to us unknown,
Being close to God by reason of His curse.
Sometimes I think that God Himself is cursed,
For all His things go wrong. We cannot guess
He is very God of God, not God of men:
We feel His power. His inhumanity;
Yet, being men, we fain would think Him good.
Since in imagination we conceive

A merciful, a gracious God of men,
It may be that our prayer and innocent life
Will shame Him into goodness in the end.
Meantime His vengeance is upon us; so,
My blessing and God's curse be with you all.

ECLOGUES

THE FEAST OF ST. HILARY

BERTRAM, LIONEL, SANDY, CYRIL, VIVIAN

BERTRAM
Your evolution, still so crude
In civic life, prefers sit
In murky air of muslin stewed
With soot and sulphur of the pit.

LIONEL
Why, this is only London's own
Appurtenance in Janiveer
And winter months — a want of tone,
A jaundice of the atmosphere.

VIVIAN
And very winter cheerful folk,
Six millions powerless to escape.
Upon this clammy muslin choke,
This filthy air of sodden crape.

Expecting no imperial cure
From any corporate King Log
They undergo it, forte et dure,
The torture of the London fog.

And though habitual croakers croak,
A metaphysical desire
Not to consume our proper smoke,
Save when the chimney goes on fire.

Through urban and suburban deeps
Sub-conscious in the minds of all.
Explains the tolerance that keeps
Our fog a hardy annual.

LIONEL

I love the fog: in every street
Shrill muffled cries and shapes forlorn,
The frosted hoof with stealthy beat.
The hollow-sounding motor-horn:

A fog that lasts till, gently wrung
By Pythian pangs, we realise
That Doomsday somewhere dawns among
The systems and the galaxies,

And ruin at the swiftest rate
The chartered destinies pursue;
While as for us, our final fate
Already fixed with small ado,

Spills on our heads no wrathful cup.
Nor wrecks us on a fiery shore,
But leaves us simply swallowed up
In London fog for evermore.

CYRIL
The admirable errantry
Of London's climate who can sing?
From fogs of filthy muslin free
Elastic as a morn of Spring,

The weather like a dazzling bride
Undid the lonely winter, threw
The casemate of the orient wide
And made the enchanted world anew.

But yesterday, so quick and so
Chromatic is the climate here —
From russet mud to silver snow,
From radiant suns to fogs austere.

LIONEL
I watched the morning yesterday
Where from the ample stair you look
Across the Park beneath the gray
Ungainly column of the Duke:

You see him like a stylite true
Impaled upon his pillar stand; —
It seems to pierce him through and through,
The rod that braves the levin-brand.

Sunlit the other column glowed

Intensely, lifting to the skies
The admiral who swept the road
Of empire clear for centuries.

Entangled on the Surrey-side
The eager day a moment hung,
Then struck in hate his ardent stride
And round the southern chimneys swung.

A silvery weft of finest lawn,
So thin, so phantom-like, became
Ethereal mystery scarcely drawn
Athwart the morning's saffron flame;

The Palace and the Abbey lost
Their character of masonry,
Transformed to glittering shadows tossed
And buoyant on a magic sea;

And park and lake and precincts old
Of Westminster were all arrayed
In spectral weeds of pearl and gold
And airy drifts of amber braid,

BERTRAM
Ghastly and foul, as Hecate's ban
Pernicious are our fogs; but sweet
And wonderful the mists that can
Imparadise a London street:

The fabrics winnowed sunbeams work
Of urban dew and smoky air;
The opalescences that lurk
In many a court and sombre square;

The tissued dawn that gems encrust,
The violet wreaths of noon, the haze
Of emerald and topaz dust
That shrouds the evening distances;

And gloom in baths of light annealed . . .

Enter **SANDY**.

LIONEL
From top to toe one travel-stain
You come! And whence?

SANDY
An outland weald
I come from, and a dateless reign

That modes and periods never touch.

BERTRAM
From Epping Forest, I'll be sworn,
The wilderness you haunt so much!

SANDY
No; from a less familiar bourne:

A Sussex chace renowned of old
Where withering innovation halts;
A tract of mingled wood and wold,
Of ragged heaths and ferny vaults.

LIONEL
St. Leonard's Forest by your shoes
Over the latchet daubed with earth!
I know it well: the Mole, the Ouse,
Arun and Adur have their birth

Among its silting springs; and there
The nightingale has never sung,
They say, so humid is the air,
So dank the woods with ivy hung.

In summer-time you lightly tread
On moss as green as emerald.
And soft as silken velvet spread
Along the forest chancel, stalled

With bowers of thorn and laurel-tree;
And roomier and loftier
Than forest aisles are wont to be,
The green groined roof of beech and fir

Admits a dulcet twilight filled
With golden motes and beryl hues.
That through the darkling thickets gild
Arun and Adur, Mole and Ouse.

SANDY
When I went out from Horsham town
A northern blast of winter's breath
Blew low across the open down

As hard as hate, as cold as death.

Close to the land the firmament
Like a camp-ceiling clung; and nigh
The eaves of the horizon, bent
Like frowning brows, the ashen sky.

Through ruined loopholes scattered wide
A pallid gleam; but as the path.
Leaving the highway, leapt aside
To gain the forest, winter's wrath,

By sheltering hedgerows doubly balked,
Became a legendary thing,
And for a while beside me walked
The very presence of the spring.

A bridge that spans a pebbled burn
The threshold of the forest is;
And there like some deedalian urn,
Or sangreal of fragrances,

A deeply sunk, a vaulted dell
Possessed the summer's inmost soul —
A captive, like the roseal smell
That haunts a seeming-empty bowl:

Though all the roses, plucked and rent,
Arc squandered, yet our essence knows
And greets the pure material scent,
Which is the spirit of the rose.

Within the forest-chancel, stalled
With bowers of evergreen and laid
With lustrous living emerald.
As rich a moss as spring displayed.

No green groined roof of fir and beech
Reflected bronze and beryl hues.
That could through darkling thickets reach
Arun and Adur, Mole and Ouse:

Unthatched, instead of summer's leaves,
A roof, with ebon rafters bare.
Allowed the light in frosted sheaves
To silver all the wintry air.

With clapping wings doves wheeled about

Between the pine-tops and the skies;
And blackbirds flitted in and out
The underwood with guttural cries;

A throstle had begun to build
Though still untimed; but loud and long
The eager storm-cock sang and filled
The forest with his splendid song;

While spring, in winter's bosom warm,
Prologued in bough and bole and root
The pregnant trance of trees that form
The summer's foliage, flower and fruit.

BERTRAM
Harvest in winter's bosom sleeps,
While time his patient .vigil keeps.

ST. VALENTINE'S DAY

ERNEST, JULIAN,

JULIAN
Virginia lives in a square;
I harbour at hand in a street:
And spring has begun over there;
So love Tike a pestilence sweet
Envenoms the neighbouring air.

ERNEST
No pestilence, Julian! Greet

The coming of Spring with delight.
Have done with your modish display
The cynic's intelligent spite
Arrives by the miriest way;
The ferment that works in the night
Of a prodigal, desolate day,

A morbid, acidulent scorn.
Inhabits the vinegared lees
In bosoms condignly forlorn—

JULIAN
In bosoms philosophy frees
From the burden to which we are born I

ERNEST

In bosoms that nothing can please,

Being empty of pleasure and sunk
In themselves; being wizened and frail
Like vats when the wine has been drunk—
Being warped and unspeakably stale
Like vats in desuetude shrunk.
Let the season and nature prevail;

Let the winepress of youth overrun; —

JULIAN

If the valves be corroded with rust,
And the power and gearing undone!

ERNEST

Empurpled with stains of the mpst
My fancy, forestalling the sun —

JULIAN

In the city we take him on trust!

ERNEST

Disheartened the fog with a glance,
And tinctured with opulent dyes
Of the lily, the rose and the raunce
The sombre, the tenebrous skies —
With the tricoloured blazon of France,
And the light of a paramour's dyes!

For this is St. Valentine's Day,
And my sweetheart came into the lane
As I went by the speediest way.
Being late for the morning train,
Diana, in sweet disarray,
The wonder of women, was fain

To see and be seen of me-first!

JULIAN

How happy to love and be loved!
How wretched is he, how accursed,
Whom destiny handles ungloved!

ERNEST

The highest encounter the worst;

For they must be sifted and proved,
While the rabble are shaken with ease
Through a wide-meshed riddle of fate.

JULIAN
O spare your proverbial pleas
And the wisdom that wiseacres prate!

ERNEST
You said that philosophy frees —

JULIAN
From a passion I would not abate

For the wealth of the world all told?
From the exquisite alchemy pain,
That tortures the dross into gold?
I spoke in a negligent vein,
For I love like the lovers of old,
Adoring a woman's disdain.

That crushes the doughtiest hope.

ERNEST
You speak like a vassal of words.
The indolent slave of a trope!
Exalt your irresolute thirds
Into fifths and their jubilant scope;
And learn of St. Valentine's birds

That love is the herald of joy.

JULIAN
The pursuivant rather of care!

ERNEST
You must brood on her beauty and cloy
Your fancy, extinguish despair
With obdurate visions; destroy
Yourself in her excellence rare;

Be buried in dreams of her worth!

JULIAN
My heart with her excellence bleeds;
My dreams of her people the earth.
And the curse is, there's nothing she needs;
She is rich and a woman of birth.

While I am the son of my deeds.

ERNEST
Achieve then a sire of renown;
Perform to the height and be great,
You have fought —

JULIAN
And defeat was my crown!
When, naked, I wrestled with fate
The destinies trampled me down: —
I fought in the van and was great,
And I won, though I wore no crown,
In the lists of the world; for fate
And the destinies trampled me down —
The myrmidons trampled me down.

SNOW

I

"Who affirms that crystals are alive?"
"I affirm it, let who will deny: —
Crystals are engendered, wax and thrive,
Wane and wither; I have seen them die.

Trust me, masters, crystals have their day,
Eager to attain the perfect norm,

Lit with purpose, potent to display
Facet, angle, colour, beauty, form.

II

Water-crystals need for flower and root
Sixty clear degrees, no less, no more;
Snow, so fickle, still in this acute
Angle thinks, and learns no other lore:

Such its life, and such its pleasure is,
'Such its art and traffic, such its gain.
Evermore in new conjunctions this
Admirable angle Lu maintain.

Crystalcraft in every flower and flake

Snow exhibits, of the welkin free;
Crystalline are crystals for the sake.
All and singular, of crystalry.

Yet does every crystal of the snow
Individualise, a seedling sown
Broadcast, but instinct with power to grow
Beautiful in beauty of its own.

Every flake with all its prongs and dints
Burns ecstatic as a new-lit star:
Men are not more diverse, finger-prints
More dissimilar than snow-flakes are.

Worlds of men and snow endure, increase.
Woven of power and passion to defy
Time and travail: only races cease,
Individual men and crystals die.

III

Jewelled shapes of snow whose feathery showers,
Fallen or falling wither at a breath,
All afraid are they, and loth as flowers
Beasts and men to tread the way to death.

Once I saw upon an object-glass,
Martyred underneath a microscope,
One elaborate snow-flake slowly pass,
Dying hard, beyond the reach of hope.

Still from shape to shape the crystal changed,
Writhing in its agony; and still.
Less and less elaborate, arranged
Potently the angle of its will.

Tortured to a simple final form,
Angles six and six divergent beams,
Lo, in death it touched the perfect norm
Verifying all its crystal dreams I

IV

Such the noble tragedy of one
Martyred snow-flake. Who can tell the fate
Heinous and uncouth of showers undone,

Fallen in cities! — showers that expiate

Errant lives from polar worlds adrift
Where the great millennial snows abide;
Castaways from mountain-chains that lift
Snowy summits in perennial pride;

Nomad snows, or snows in evil day
Born to urban ruin, to be tossed,
Trampled, shovelled, ploughed and swept away
Down the seething sewers: all the frost

Flowers of heaven melted up with lees,
Offal, recrement, but every flake
Showing to the last in fixed degrees
Perfect crystals for the crystal's sake.

V

Usefulness of snow is but a chance
Here in temperate climes with winter sent,
Sheltering earth's prolonged hibernal trance:
All utility is accident.

Sixty clear degrees the joyful snow,
Practising economy of means.
Fashions endless beauty in, and so
Glorifies the universe with scenes

Arctic and antarctic; stainless shrouds,
Ermine woven in silvery frost, attire
Peaks in every land among the clouds
Crowned with snows to catch the morning's fire.

THE TESTAMENT OF SIR SIMON SIMPLEX CONCERNING AUTOMOBILISM

That railways are inadequate appears
Indubitable now. For sixty years
Their comfort grew until the train de luxe
Arrived, arousing in conducted Cook's,
And other wholesale, tourists, an envious smart
For here they recognised the perfect art
And science of land-travel. Now we sing
A greater era, hail a happier Spring.
The motor-car reveals ineptitude

In railway-trains; and travellers conclude
The railway is archaic: strictly true,
Although the reason sounds as false as new; —
Railways are democratic, vulgar, laic;
And who can doubt Democracy's archaic?
The railway was the herald and the sign,
And powerful agent in the swift decline
Of Europe and the West. The future sage
Will blame sententiously the railway age,
Preachers upon its obvious vices pounce,
And poets, wits and journalists pronounce
The nineteenth century in prose and rhyme
The most unhappy period of time.
That nations towering once in pomp and pride
Of monarchs, rank and breeding, should subside
To one dead undistinguishable horde
Sans sceptre, mitre, coronet and sword.
Reverting to a pithecoidal state
May be the purpose of recurrent fate;
But that such folks should to themselves appear
Progressing toward a great millennial year
Is just the bitter-sweet, the chilly-hot.
The subtle metaphysic of the plot.

The last age saw the last stage of the fit
That pestered, when the Roman Empire split.
The catalytic centuries: the strange
Insanity that fed on secular change;
The general paralysis of men
That ended in the railway and the wen
Called London: from the Tiber to the Thames,
From dreaming empire to delirious aims
That move the laughter of the careless fates,
And effervesce in socialistic pates.

But convalescence with the car begins
And petrol expiates our railway sins.
Before we know we shall with joy behold
A world as sane as any world of old;
From labour and electoral problems free,
A world the fibre of whose health shall be,
No Will to be the Mob, but mastering all,
A Will to be the Individual;
For every Mob exhales a poisonous breath,
And Socialism is decadence, is death:
The Mob expropriates, degrades, destroys;
The Individual conquers, makes, enjoys.
Not till the motor was the contrast plain,

Because the separate classes of the train
Deceived us with a choice of company;
And, when he liked, the tame celebrity,
The genius, man of wealth, aristocrat.
By means of tips through any journey sat
In cornered state; or with sufficient pelf
Could purchase a compartment for himself.
He rather would have deemed himself a snob
Than that the train could turn him into Mob,
Till automotion's privacy and pride
Exposed the grossness of the railway ride;
For 'twas the freedom of the motor-car
That showed how tyrannous the railways are.

To go by train from one place to another
You have to brave the station's smoke and smother
The train derides you there; 'twill never come
To pick you up, nor turn, to see you home,
A single wheel; the getting under way,
The true vexation of a holiday,
The stolid train permits you to deplore;
But with your automobile at the door —
Why, there you are, nor need you stir a foot,
Man and portmanteau instantly en route!
You buy a ticket if you go by train
At some offensive loophole, which you gain
After prolonged attendance in a queue —
Whatever class you take, a motley crew:
And to await one's turn, like patient Job,
Unites one with a vengeance to the Mob.
Then you may miss the train; but must wait
Its advent and departure prompt or late.
The motor soothes, the railway racks, your nerves;
The train commands, the automobile serves.
The automobile nurses all caprice,
And gives the longest life a second lease;
Indulges indolence, and even in me
Increases individuality.
I thought and many my opinion shared
That the deceased politic who declared
That all were Socialists, had told, perhaps,
A fib, exploited in a studied lapse
Of platform declamation as a sop
To catch erratic voters on the hop,
The strained politeness of a caustic mind,
A dead-lift effort to say something kind.
'Twas more than that: not only had we learned
To suffer Socialism; our souls discerned

A something fine about it; egoists even
Perceived therein at last a mundane heaven.

"Life is a railway journey", genius thought —
(The erring genius very cheaply bought
With gilded apples of Asphaltites) —
"Thieves bearing swag, and poets sprouting bays,
The ring, the cabinet, scortatory dames,
Bishops, sectarians of a myriad names,
Bankers and brokers, merchants, mendicants,
Booked in the same train like a swarm of ants;
First, second, third, class, mass and mob expressed
Together to the Islands of the Blest—
Each passenger provided with a groat
To pass the Stygian stile for Charon's boat.
Or broad or narrow as the gauge may run,
None leaves the track without disaster; none
Escapes a single stoppage on the way;
And none arrives before his neighbour may.
In the guard's van my sacred luggage knocks
Against the tourist's traps, the bagman's box;
And people with inferior aims to mine
Partake the rapid transit of the line.
But this is culture of the social school.
And teaches me to lead my life by rule
Empirical, of positive descent
And altruistic self-embezzlement.
Life is a railway journey: I rejoice
That folk whose purpose, visage, clothes and voice
Offend me will continue to offend
In the same train until the journey's end".

So spoke the genius in pathetic rage. —
The socialistic and the railway age
Were certainly coeval; machinery too
Equated communism; and every new
Development of electricity
Was welcomed by the Mob with three times three,
Convinced the world at last was through the wood —
Right through to Universal Brotherhood!

Conceive it: — Universal Brotherhood,
With everybody feeble, kind and good!
I, even I, Sir Simon Simplex, know
The world would end to-day if that were so.
What spur does man require, what stinging zest
To do still better than his level best?
Why, enemies; and if he has them not

He must unearth and beat them till they're hot;
For only enmity can train and trounce
The cortex and the muscle to an ounce.
Let Socialists deny, mistaking peace,
That only with the world will warfare cease;
When we behold the battle-flags unfurled
We know the fates phlebotomise the world,
And alternate with peace's patent pill,
The old heroic cure for every ill.

Life was a railway journey; foe and friend,
Infected with nostalgy of the end,
Awaited patiently the crack of doom;
But thank the powers that be, the motor boom,
Predestined to postpone the judgment-day,
Arrived in time to show a better way.
And when the automobile came we found
Our incorrupt opinion safe and sound,
Inoculated only by the schism,
For ever proof against all Socialism.
The motor stops the decadence: not all
Are in the same train with the prodigal,
The Christian scientist, the souteneur,
The Gothamite, the man from anywhere,
Domestic Gill and idiomatic Jack,
The wheedling knave, the sneak, the hectoring quack;
The man of broader mind and farther goal
Is not entrained with Lubin Littlesoul;
Your gentleman by birth with quickened sense,
Refined requirements and abundant pence,
And men of faculty and swelling aim
Who conquer riches, power, position, fame,
Are not entrained with loafers, quibblers, cranks,
Nor with the Mob who never leave the ranks,
With plodding dullness, unambitious ease,
And discontented incapacities.

Goodwill is in the blood, in you and me,
And most in men of wealth and pedigree;
So rich and poor, men, women, age and youth
Imagined some ingredient of truth
In Socialistic faith that there could be
A common basis of equality.
But now we know and by the motor swear
The prepossession was as false as fair:
Men are not equal; no two intellects
Are of a calibre; desires, defects,
Powers, aptitudes, are never on a par.

No more than finger-prints and noses are.
And on my soul and conscience I maintain
Political equality's as vain
As personal: for instance, I would place
The franchise on a principle of race,
And give the Saxon's forward reach a felt
Prepotence o'er the backward-glancing Celt;
And if his chauffeur counts as one, why then
Sir Simon Simplex should be reckoned ten.
I call Democracy archaic, just
As manhood suffrage is atavic lust
For folkmotes of the prime, whose analogue
In travel was the train, a passing vogue:
The automobile put an end to that,
And left Democracy as fallen and flat
As railway-stock. Wealth and the crafty hand
That gathers wealth had always at command
Horse-carriages for private travel, but
The pace had got beyond that leisured rut;
Class, mass and mob for fifty years and more
Had all to travel in the jangling roar
Of railways, the nomadic caravan
That stifled individual mind in man,
Till automobilism arose at last!
Now with the splendid periods of the past
Our youthful century is proudly linked;
And things that Socialism supposed extinct,
Degree, nobility and noble strife,
A form, a style, a privacy in life
Will reappear; and, crowning nature's plan.
The individual and the gentleman
In England reassume his lawful place
And vindicate the greatness of the race.

THE CAKE OF MITHRIDATES

Quenched is the fire on autumn's hearth,
The ingle vacant, hushed the song;
But the resolved, consistent earth,
And nature, tolerant and strong.

Serenely wait the ordered change
Of times and tides. Ten thousand years
Of day and night, the scope and range
Of liberal seasons; smiles and tears

Of June and April; brumal storm,
Autumnal calm, and flower and fruit:
These are the rich content, the form
Of nature's mind; these constitute

The academe and discipline,
The joust and knightly exercise,
The culture of the earth wherein
The earth's profound composure lies.

The wisdom of the earth excels
The craft and skill of every age
Witness the tale the Persian tells
Of Mithridates, king and mage: —

The whole divan extolled his powers
They said the soil revered him so:
That, if he planted sawdust, flowers
Of every hue would promptly grow.

"So be it!" quoth the King of kings;
Bring hither sweepings of the street,
Chaff, sawdust, money, jewels, rings,
And fifty grains of summer wheat".

He sowed them in a fertile bed,
And set a guard about the plot
Both day and night: "Although", he said,
"The earth is honest, men are not".

The wheat betimes began to grow.
In shame as in a mordant steeped,
The viziers, sulking in a row,
Beheld at length the harvest reaped.

Said then the King, "A sheaf! Proceed:
Thresh, winnow, grind it, bolt and bake.
And bring with all convenient speed
Of leavened bread a goodly cake.

"For you, my worthy viziers — come!
The marvellous crops you promised me?"
The whole perturbed divan, as dumb
As oysters, felt indeed at sea.

"Ha!" cried the King, "when shall we laugh
At prodigies great nature grants
Almighty monarchs? Fruit of chaff.

Where is it? Where, my sawdust-plants?

"The vine and vintage of my gold?
My silver-bushes, where are they?
My coin should yield a hundred-fold
By nature's lavish usury!

"My fragrant banks of posied rings
Where diamonds blossom, show me; show
In arbours where the bulbul sings
A branch of budding rubies glow.

"My jewel-orchards, money-shrubs?
Perhaps they've sprouting underground?
My cash, at least, among the grubs—
My cash and gems! Let them be found!

"Dig, viziers, dig!" The viziers dug:
Among the deep roots of the grain.
With here an earthworm, there a slug
They found the treasure, sowed in vain.

And all the sweepings of the streets,
The chaff, the rubbish? Like a jest
Forgiven, forgotten I So discreet
Is nature's kindly alkahest.

Then every vizier lost his nerve.
Expecting death, a prompt despatch.
But Mithridates said, "Observe
How great the soil is: bulbuls hatch

"The cuckoo's eggs, whereas the earth
Ignores the costliest stone to feed
With chosen fare and bring to birth
The soul of any honest seed.

"The earth is true and harbours not
Imposture; all your flattering lies
Are buried in this garden-plot;
Be genuine if you would be wise

With that the baker, breathing spice,
Produced the cake hot from the fire.
And every vizier ate a slice
Resolving to be less a liar.

THE LUTANIST

The harvests of purple and gold
Are garnered and trodden; dead leaves
To-morrow will carpet the wold;
And the arbours and sylvan eaves
Dismantled, no welcome extend;
The bowers and the sheltering eaves
Will witness to-morrow the end
Of their stained, of their sumptuous leaves,
While tempests apparel the wold
In their cast-off crimson and gold.

But I of abundance to be
Think only, the corn and the wine,
The manifold wealth of the sea
And the harvest-home of the mine.
Decay and the fall of leaf,
Lost lives in the tenebrous mine,
Disaster, disconsolate grief
Molest not the corn and the wine,
The infinite wealth of the sea
And the bountiful harvests to be.

For beneath are the heavens and above,
And time is a silken yoke;
My lute is my friend; and I love
A beautiful maid of my folk —
A marvel to see and adore,
Astounding her foes and her folk
With silence and exquisite lore
Of youth and its delicate yoke.
With wonderful wisdom in love.
And the music beneath and above.

I think how her beauty would kill
A lover less ardent than I,
I faint and my heart stands still
In the street when she passes by;
My lute, I bid it be dumb: —
"Hush, for my love goes by!
O hush, or she may not come!
A lover less ardent than I
Her beauty might palsy, might kill!
Lute-strings, heart-strings, be still!

But when she has passed a spell

Delivers my voice and my lute;
My songs and my melodies well
Like fountains; like clustery of fruit
My fantasy ripens; my rhymes.
With savour of wayside fruit
And sweet as aerial chimes
Of flower-bells, ring to my lute;
Like fountains my melodies well
When the thought of her works like a spell.

She walks and the emerald lawn
Is jewelled at every tread;
Like the burning tresses of dawn
The virgin gold of her head
Illumines the land and the sea;
From her glittering feet to her head
Is the essence of being — is she
Who walks with a magical tread
As she dazzles the eyes of dawn
And jewels the grass-green lawn.

Though the harvests of purple and gold
Are garnered, and fallen leaves
To-morrow will carpet the wold,
I think how the sylvan eaves
A welcome in summer extend,
How the bowers and the sheltering eaves
Will mantle in summer and bend
With their bloom and their burden of leaves,
And autumn apparel the wold
In harvests of purple and gold.

ST. MICHAEL'S MOUNT

St. Michael's Mount, the tidal isle,
In May with daffodils and lilies
Is kirtled gorgeously a while
As ne'er another English hill is:
About the precipices cling
The rich renascence robes offspring.

Her gold and silver, nature's gifts,
The prodigal with both hands showers:
O not in patches, not in drifts
But round and round, a mount of flowers —
Of lilies and of daffodils,

The envy of all other hills.

And on the lofty summit looms
The castle; none could build or plan it.
The foursquare foliage springs and blooms,
The piled elaborate flower of granite,
That not the sun can wither; no,
Nor any tempest overthrow.

TWO DOGS

Two dogs on Bournemouth beach: a mongrel, one,
With spaniel plainest on the palimpsest,
The blur of muddled stock; the other, bred,
With tapering muzzle, rising brow, strong jaw —
A terrier to the tail's expressive tip,
Magnetic, nimble, endlessly alert.

The mongrel, wet and shivering, at my feet
Deposited a wedge of half-inch board,
A foot in length and splintered at the butt;
Withdrew a yard and crouched in act to spring,
While to and fro between his wedge and me
The glancing shuttle of his eager look
A purpose wove. The terrier, ears a-cock,
And neck one curve of sheer intelligence,
Stood sentinel: no sound, no movement, save
The mongrel's telegraphic eyes, bespoke
The object of the canine pantomime.

I Stooped to grasp the wedge, knowing the game;
But like a thing uncoiled the mongrel snapped
It off, and promptly set it out again,
The terrier at his quarters, every nerve
Waltzing inside his lithe rigidity.

"More complex than I thought! Again I made
To seize the wedge; again the mongrel won,
Whipped off the jack, relaid it, crouched and watched,
The terrier at attention all the time.
I won the third bout; ere the mongrel snapped
His toy, I stayed my hand: he halted, half
Across the neutral ground, and in the pause
Of doubt I seized the prize. A vanquished yelp
From both; and then intensest vigilance.

Together, when I tossed the wedge, they plunged
Before it reached the sea. The mongrel, out
Among the waves, and standing to them, meant
Heroic business; but the terrier dodged
Behind, adroitly scouting in the surf,
And seized the wedge, rebutted by the tide,
In shallow water, while the mongrel searched
The English Channel on his hind-legs poised.
The terrier laid the trophy at my feet:
And neither dog protested when I took
The wedge: the overture of their marine
Diversion had been played out once for all.

A second match the reckless mongrel won,
Vanishing twice under the heavy surf,
Before he found and brought the prize to land.
Then for an hour the aquatic sport went on,
And still the mongrel took the heroic role,
The terrier hanging deftly in the rear.
Sometimes the terrier when the mongrel found
Betrayed a jealous scorn, as who should say.
"Your heroes always a vulgarian! Pah!"
But when the mongrel missed, after a fight
With such a sea of troubles, and saw the prize
Grabbed by the terrier in an inch of surf,
He seemed entirely satisfied, and watched
With more pathetic vigilance the cast
That followed.

"Once a passion, mongrel, this
Retrieving of a stick", I told the brute,
"Has now become a vice with you. Go home!
Wet to the marrow and palsied with the cold,
You won't give in, and, good or bad, you've earned
My admiration. Go home now and get warm,
And the best bone in the pantry As I talked
I stripped the water from his hybrid coat,
Laughed arid made much of him — which mortified
The funking terrier.

"I'm despised, it seems!"
The terrier thought. "My cleverness (my feet
Are barely wet!) beside the mongrel's zeal
Appears timidity. This biped's mad
To pet the stupid brute. Yap I Yah!" He seized
The wedge and went; and at his heels at once,
Without a thought of me, the mongrel trudged.

Along the beach, smokers of cigarettes.
All sixpenny-novel-readers to a man,
Attracted Master Terrier. Again the wedge.
Passed to the loyal mongrel, was teed with care;
Again the fateful overture began.
Upon the fourth attempt, and not before,
And by a feint at that, the challenged youth
(Most equable, be sure, of all the group:
Allow the veriest dog to measure men!)
Secured the soaked and splintered scrap of deal.
Thereafter, as with me, the game progressed,
The breathless, shivering mongrel, rushing out
Into the heavy surf, there to be tossed
And tumbled like a floating bunch of kelp.
While gingerly the terrier picked his steps
Strategic in the rear, and snapped the prize
Oftener than his more adventurous, more
Romantic, more devoted rival did.
The uncomfortable moral glares at one!
And, further, in the mongrel's wistful mind
A primitive idea darkly wrought:
Having once lost the prize in the overture
With his bipedal rival, he felt himself
In honour and in conscience bound to plunge
For ever after it at the winner's will.
But the smart terrier was an Overdog,
And knew a trick worth two of that. He thought—
If canine cerebration works like ours,
And I interpret canine mind aright —
"Let men and mongrels worry and wet their coats!
I use my brains and choose the better part.
Quick-witted ease and self-approval lift
Me miles above this anxious cur, absorbed,
Body and soul, in playing a game I win
Without an effort. And yet the mongrel seems
The happier dog. How's that? Belike, the old
Compensatory principle again.
I have pre-eminence and conscious worth;
And he has power to fling himself away
For anything or nothing. Men and dogs,
What an unfathomable world it is!"

THE WASP

Once as I went by rail to Epping Street,
Both windows being open, a wasp flew in;

Through the compartment swung and almost out
Scarce seen, scarce heard; but dead against the pane
Entitled "Smoking," did the train's career
Arrest her passage. Such a wonderful
Impervious transparency, before
That palpitating moment, had never yet
Her airy voyage thwarted. Undismayed,
With diligence incomparable, she sought
An exit, till the letters like a snare
Entangled her; or else the frosted glass
And signature indelible appeared
The key to all the mystery: there she groped,
And flirted petulant wings, and fiercely sang
A counter-spell against the sorcery,
The sheer enchantment that inhibited
Her access to the world — her birthright there!
So visible, and so beyond her reach I
Baffled and raging like a tragic queen,
She left at last the stencilled tablet; roamed
The pane a while to cool her regal ire,
Then tentatively touched the window-frame:
Sure footing still, though rougher than the glass;
Dissimilar in texture, and so obscure!

Perplexed now by opacity with foot and wing
She coasted up and down the wood and worked
Her wrath to passion-point again. Then from the frame
She slipped by chance into the open space
Left by the lowered sash; — the world once more
In sight I She paused; she closed her wings, and felt
The air with learned antennae for the smooth
Resistance that she knew now must belong
To such mysterious transparences.
No foothold? Down she fell — six inches down! —
Hovered a second, dazed and dubious still;
Then soared away a captive queen set free,

THE THAMES EMBANKMENT

As gray and dank as dust and ashes slaked
With wash of urban tides the morning lowered;
But over Chelsea Bridge the sagging sky
Had colour in it — blots of faintest bronze,
The stains of daybreak. Westward slabs of light
From vapour disentangled, sparsely glazed
The panelled firmament; but vapour held

The morning captive in the smoky east.
At lowest ebb the tide on either bank
Laid bare the fat mud of the Thames, all pinched
And scalloped thick with dwarfish surges. Cranes,
Derricks and chimney-stalks of the Surrey-side,
Inverted shadows, in the motionless,
Dull, leaden mirror of the channel hung:
Black flags of smoke broke out, and in the dead
Sheen of the water hovered underneath,
As in the upper region, listlessly,
Across the viaduct trailing plumes of steam,
The trains clanked in and out.

Slowly the sun
Undid the homespun swathing of the clouds,
And splashed his image on the northern shore —
A thing extravagantly beautiful:
The glistening, close-grained canvas of the mud
Like hammered copper shone, and all about
The burning centre of the mirror'd orbs
Illimitable depth of silver fire
Harmonious beams the overtones of light.
Suffused the emboss'd, metallic river bank.
Woven of rainbows a dewdrop can dissolve
And packed with power a simple lens can wield,
The perfect, only source of beauty, light
Reforms uncouthest shapelessness and turns
Decoloured refuse into ornament;
The leafless trees that lined the vacant street
Had all their stems picked out in golden scales,
Their branches carved in ebony; and shed
Around them by the sanction of the morn
In lieu of leaves each wore an aureole.
Barges at anchor, barges stranded, hulks
Ungainly, in the unshorn beams and rich
Replenished planet of a winter sun,
Appeared ethereal, and about to glide
On high adventure chartered, swift away
For regions undiscovered.

Huddled wharfs
A while, and then once more a reach of Thames
Visibly flowing where the sun and wind
Together caught the current. Quays and piers
To Vauxhall Bridge, and there the Baltic Wharf
Exhibited its wonders: figureheads
Of the old wooden walls on gate and post —
Colossal torsos, bulky bosoms thrown

Against the storm, sublime uplifted eyes
Telling the stars. As white as ghosts
They overhung the way, usurping time
With carved memorials of the past. Forlorn
Elysium of the might of England!

Gulls,
Riparian scavengers, arose and wheeled
About my head, for morsels begging loud
With savage cries that piercingly reverbed
The tempest's dissonance. Birds in themselves
Unmusical and uninventive ape
Impressive things with mocking undesigned:
The eagle's bark mimics the crashing noise
That shakes his eyry when the thunder roars;
And chanticleer's imperious trumpet-call
Re-echoes round the world his ancestor's
Barbaric high-wrought challenge to the dawn;
But birds of homely feather and tuneful throat,
With music in themselves and masterdom,
To beauty turn obsessive sight and sound:
The mounting larks, compact of joyful fire,
Render the coloured sunlight into song;
Adventurous and impassioned nightingales
Transmute the stormy equinox they breast
With courage high, for hawthorn thickets bound
When spring arrives, into the melody
That floods the forest aisles; the robin draws
Miraculously from the rippling brook
The red wine of his lay; blackbird and thrush,
Prime-artists of the woodland, proudly take
All things sonorous for their province, weave
The gold-veined thunder and the crystal showers,
The winds, the rivers and the choir of birds
In the rich strains of their chromatic score.

By magic mechanism the weltering clouds
Re-grouped themselves in continents and isles
That diapered the azure firmament;
And sombre chains of cumulus, outlined
In ruddy shade along the house-tops loomed,
Phantasmal alp on alp. The sunbeams span
Chaotic vapour into cosmic forms,
And juggled in the sky, with hoods of cloud
As jesters twirl on sticks their booby-caps —
The potent sunbeams, that had fished the whole
Enormous mass of moisture from the sea,
Kneaded, divided and divided, wrought

And turned it to a thousand fantasies
Upon the ancient potter's wheel, the earth.

THE ARISTOCRAT OF THE ROAD

More than one way of walking? Verily;
But, for the art of walking, only one.
Beginners in the ambulative art,
As in all art, are immethodical:
Your want of method, rightly understood.
Is faculty, and not its absence; style
Adventurous of genius; say, a gift;
Immethod, necessary handicap
Upon originality, that loses
Matches many on time or weight, but beats
The winner virtually. The crammer's wiles.
And royal roads to knowledge, short-cuts, keys.
And time-and-labour-saving mechanism
Beset the ambulative acolyte;
But true originality in art
Would not at first, even if it could, possess
Impeccable technique; and your foredoomed
Pedestrian errs designedly (if one
Whose privilege it is to deviate
Can ever be arraigned for trespass) bent
On quitting, jeopardy or none, the old
Immediately seductive methods blazed
By trained precursors in pedestrial art.

At first then the prospective walker, rash
As any hero, dedicates himself
To chance. A vagabond upon the earth
He leads a life uncertain: art and craft
Pedalian suffer secret chrysalid
Probations and adventures ere they gain
The ultimate imago of complete
Pedestrianism. Through gross suburban miles
And over leagues of undistinguished ground
He plods, he tramps. Utilitarian thoughts
Of exercise and health extenuate
The dullness of the duty; he persuades
Himself he likes it; finds, where none exist.
Amazing qualities; and tires his limbs.
His thought, his fancy, o'er and o'er again.
But in the dismal watches of the night
He knows it all delusion; beauty, none.

Nor pleasure in it; ennui only — eased
By speculation on the wayside-inn,
Or country-town hotel where lunch permits
An hour's oblivion of his self-imposed,
His thriftless drudgery. Despair! — And life?
Worth picking from the gutter? No; not worth
The stooping for! Natheless, a walker born,
He takes the road next day; steps out once more,
As if the world were just begun, and he,
Sole monarch; plods the suburb, tramps the waste —
Again returning baffled and dismayed.

He tries a comrade. Worse and worse! — for that,
In high pedestrianism, turns out to be
A double misery, a manacled
Contingence with vexation. Walking-tours?
Belletrists crack them up. He takes one: — lo,
A sheer atrocity! A man may like
To drink, but who would quench next morning's drouth,
Unholy though it be, with torture forte
Et dure in gallon draughts when by his bed
A hair gleams of the dog that bit him! Tours
Pedestrious? Madness, like the poet's who thought
To write a thousand sonnets at the rate
Of three a day! And this the tale of years!

Forth from his travail and despair at last,
Crash through his plodding apparatus, breaks
The dawn of art. He recollects a mile,
Or half a mile that pleased him; a furlong here,
And there a hundred yards; or an hour's march
Over some curve of the world when everything
Above him and about him from the zenith
To the sky-edge, and radiant from his feet
Toward every cardinal point, put off the veil,
Becoming evident as guilt or love, as things
They cannot hide: — becoming him,
And he becoming them; and all his past
And all his future wholly what they are,
The very form and meaning of the earth
Itself. And at these times he recollects,
And in these places, how his thoughts were clear
As crystal, deeper than the sea, as swift
As light— the pulse, the bosom and the zone
Of beauty infinite. And then and there
Whatever he imagined took at once
A bodily shape; and nought conceived or done
Since life began appeared irrational,

Wanton or needless. Since, the world and fate,
Material functions of each other, apt
As syllables of power and magic mind
In some self-reading riddle, as fracted bits
In self-adjusting instruments that play
Unheard ethereal music of the spheres,
Assumed their places equably; all things
Fell duly into line and dressed their ranks.

Thus art begins, as sudden as a star
In some unconstellated tract of space,
Where two extinct long-wandering orbs collide
And smite into each other and become
A lamp of glory, no crepuscular
Uncertainty, no interval between
The old misfortune and the new delight.
And thus at once the plodder of the waste
Attains utility and finds himself
Aristocrat and patron of the road;
The artisan, an artist — aristocrat
And artist being over synonymes.
All vagabondage, all bohemianism,
All errantry, the unlicked, chrysalid
Condition of aristocracy and art,
Cut off for ever, the proud pedestrian free
Of the world, walks only now in picked resorts.
And can without a chart, without a guide,
Discover lands richer than El Dorado,
Sweeter than Beulah, and with ease
Ascend secluded mountains more delectable
Than height in ancient pilgrimages famed,
Or myth-clad hills, or summits of romance.
Old traversed roads he traverses again,
Untroubled; nothing new he sees
Except the stretch of pleasure-ground, like one
Who turns the leaves o'er of a tedious book,
Careless of verbiage, to reperuse
The single page inspired; in regions new
He goes directly to his own like beasts
That never miss the way; and having marked
A province with the beauties of his choice,
In them atone he walks, lord of the world.

RAIL AND ROAD

March Many-weathers, bluff and affable,

The usher and the pursuivant of Spring,
Had sent His North wind blaring through the world —
A mundane wind that held the earth, and puffed
The smoke of urban fire and furnace far
Afield. An ashen canopy of cloud,
The dense immobled sky, high-pitched above
The wind's terrestrial office, overhung
The city when the morning train drew out.
Leaping along the land from town to town,
Its iron lungs respired its breath of steam,
Its resonant flanges, and its vertebral
Loose-jointed carcase of a centipede
Gigantic, hugged and ground the parallel
Adjusted metals of its destined way
With apathetic fatalism, the mark
Of all machinery. — From Paddington
To Basingstoke the world seemed standing still:
Nothing astir between the firmaments
Except the aimless tumult of the wind,
And clanging travail of the ponderous train
In labour with its journey on the smooth,
The includible, the shining rails.

But prompt at Basingstoke an interlude
Began: a reckless youth, possessed with seven
Innocuous devils of self-consciousness
Primeval, bouncing in irruptively,
Lusty-juvenus-wise, annexed the whole
Compartment — as a pendant to the earth.
Already his! Wind-shaven, ruddy: hunched
And big: all knees and knuckles: with a mouth
That opened like a portal; fleshy chops
And turned-up nose widespread, the signature
Of jollity: a shapeless, elvish skull;
His little pig's eyes in their sockets soused
But simmering merrily: just twenty years;
One radiation of nervous energy:
A limber tongue and most unquenchable,
Complacent blaze of indiscretion, soft
As a night-light in a nursery. "Where away?"
Quoth he: and "Hang the weather! I've seen worse,
In my time, for the season". Then: Did we think
The train was doing thirty or forty miles
An hour? Sometimes, by instinct, he could tell
To a mile the rate at which a train went.
This morning, for a wonder, he couldn't trust
His judgment in the matter annoying! — Still
A man's form varied, and we must excuse

His inability to gauge our speed.
Good golf about here, — very! Did play?
And, by the by, talking of golf, he did
A brilliant thing just now missing the train
At Farnham on the other line, instead
Of waiting for the next, he tramped across
To Basingstoke, "Some decent tale of miles;
His destination being Winchester,
Either line suited, —see? The weather, — yes,
The weather; — healthy, of course; — your moist cold kills;
Your dry cold cures to-day it seemed as cold, —
But that must be the wind; in sheltered roads
It smelt like Spring: — to-morrow, — who could tell
To-morrow's weather? — a funny climate, ours!
Was that a cow there, or a — yes, a cow.
He didn't know how we regarded it,
But he, for his part, took it that the hand
That rocked the cradle ruled the world: to drop
A signature into a ballot-box
Would make no earthly! (Slang, ellipitical.)
Although we must remember, all of us,
This rocking of the cradle was out of date;
But that he wouldn't canvass: — we were to mind
There must be no mistake; women were women
All the world to nothing: and — mark him — if
They had political enfranchisement,
No one could say — no one at all! — what might
And mightn't happen: not a doubt of that.
Getting along more quickly: forty miles,
He thought: or less, perhaps. He meant to lunch
At Winchester: then hire a trap and drive . . .
"Instanter to the devil," someone sighed.
All this, and further, an infinitude
Of dislocated prattle, with a smile
Indelible, and such a negligent
Absorbition* in self that no appeal,
Except a sheer affront, abuse, or blow,
Could have revealed remotely any gleam
Or shade, to him apparent, of his own
Insipid and grotesque enormity!
When time, distemper or disaster sap
Such individuals, and they see themselves,
In facets of disrupted character,
As others sec them, stupid and absurd,
How bad the quarter of an hour must be!
Natheless there are extant a hearty breed,
Incorrigibly cheerful, who behold
Themselves for ever in the best of lights.

And by the pipe and bowl of Old King Cole
They have the best of it! To see ourselves
As others see us may be good enough;
But to love others in their vanities,
And to portray the glorious counterfeit—
In sympathetic ink that sympathy
Alone can read aright, — why that's a gift
Vouchsafed to genius of the rarest strain!
At Lyndhurst-road the coach for Lyndhurst took
The turnpike at its best commercial pace.
And there the sun burst out with moted beams
In handfuls, clenched like sheaves of thunderbolts.
The riven clouds, of homespun slashed and gored.
Displayed through unhemmed slits the turquoise sky,—
As tender as damsel's bosom-thoughts.
Across the forest's swarthy-purple ridge
A sparse shower twinkled: but the broken bulk
Of vapour, by the sunbeams bundled up.
Slipped o'er the sky-edge and was no more seen.
Like a lithe weapon by gigantic hands
In pastance wielded, keen the brandished wind
Whistled about us all the uphill way
To Lyndhurst, where lofty church o'erlooks
The forest's metes and bounds, its modish spire
A landmark far and wide. But in the glebes
And garden-closes ancient houses — thatched.
Of post-and-panel, and with arching eaves
About their high and deep-set windows— peer
Occultly out of many centuries.
An old-world use and wont, the neighbourhood
And venue of the place are everywhere
Presumptive, — in the High Street, new and raw
As in the sylvan faubourgs; for a gust
Of burning log and faggot importunes
The passer-by — the forest's bitter-sweet
Aroma, as it turns to genial warmth
And toothsome savour for the villager.

*This word has fallen out of use; but having it we might employ it. Its doublet, " absorption," could be relegated to physics, etc. and " absorbition" kept for mental engrossment The dictionaries lay the stress on the penultimate; but in restoring "absorbition" to the language, I place the main accent on the second syllable.—J. D.

SONG FOR THE TWENTY-FOURTH OF MAY

I

The character and strength of us
Who conquer everywhere,
We sing the English of it thus,
And bid the world beware;
We bid the world beware
The perfect heart and will,
That dare the utmost men may dare
And follow freedom still.
Sea-room, land-room, ours, my masters, ours.
Hand in hand with destiny, and first among the Powers!
Our boasted Ocean Empire, sirs, we boast of it again.
Our Monarch, and our Rulers, and our
Women, and our Men!

II

The pillars of our Empire stand
In unforgotten graves;
We built dominion on the land,
And greatness on the waves:
Our Empire on the waves,
Established firm and sure.
And founded deep in ocean's caves
While honour shall endure.
Sea-room, land-room, honourably ours.
Hand in hand with destiny and first among the Powers!
Our boasted Ocean Empire, sirs, we boast of it again,
Our ancient Isles, our Lands afar, and all our loyal Men!

III

Our flag, on every wind unfurled.
Proclaims from sea to sea
A future and a nobler world
Where men and thoughts are free:
Our men, our thoughts are free:
Our wars are waged for peace;
We stand in arms for liberty
Till bonds and bondage cease.
Sea-room, land-room, ours, appointed ours,
Conscious of our calling and the first among the Powers!
Our boasted Ocean Sovereignty, again and yet again!
Our Counsel, and our Conduct, and our
Armaments and Men!

John Davidson was born at Barrhead, East Renfrewshire on 11th April 1857, the son of Alexander Davidson, an Evangelical Union minister and Helen née Crocket of Elgin.

In 1862 the family moved to Greenock and Davidson began his education at Highlanders' Academy. From there he began his career, aged a mere 13, at the chemical laboratory of Walker's Sugarhouse refinery. A year later he returned to Highlander's, this time as a pupil teacher.

During his later employment at the Public Analysts' Office, 1870–71 he developed a keen interest in science which later became an important characteristic of his poetry. He returned once again to the Highlander's Academy, this time for four years, in 1872, again as a pupil teacher. In 1876 he spent a year at Edinburgh University before his first scholastic employment at Alexander's Charity, Glasgow which led to short periods of employment at various other schools over the following half a dozen years.

This led to a stint at Morrison's Academy in Crieff (1885–88), and in a private school at Greenock (1888–89).

In 1885 Davidson married Margaret McArthur and the marriage produced two children, Alexander (born in 1887) and Menzies (born in 1889).

Davidson's first published work was 'Bruce, A Chronicle Play', written in the Elizabethan style, and published by a local Glasgow imprint in 1886. Four other plays quickly followed; 'Smith, A Tragic Farce' (1888), 'An Unhistorical Pastoral' (1889), 'A Romantic Farce' (1889), and then the somewhat brilliant pantomime 'Scaramouch in Naxos' (1889).

By now he was very much immersed in literature and, in 1889, he ventured to London where he frequented the famous Fleet Street pub 'Ye Olde Cheshire Cheese' and joined the 'Rhymers' Club', a poets group that was based there.

Davidson was a prolific and hard-working writer. As well as his plays he wrote for the Speaker, the Glasgow Herald, and several other papers. He also wrote and had published several novels and tales, with perhaps the best being 'Perfervid' (1890).

With his reputation gradually providing an income he was also able to explore his true medium; Verse. 'In a Music Hall and Other Poems' (1891) together with 'Fleet Street Eclogues' (1893) were ample proof that he possessed a quite rare, genuine and distinctive poetic gift. Praise came from his peers including George Gissing and WB Yeats who wrote that it was: 'An example of a new writer seeking out new subject matter, new emotions'.

Davidson now turned further and further towards verse. In 1894 he published his most popular volume, 'Ballads and Songs' (1894), and this was followed by a further 'Fleet Street Eclogues' (Second Series) (1896) and by 'New Ballads' (1897) and 'The Last Ballad' (1899).

Davidson was a prolific writer. Besides the works cited, he wrote many other works including, 'The Wonderful Mission of Earl Lavender' (1895), a novel which extends his literary canon to flagellation erotica. He also contributed an introduction to Shakespeare's Sonnets (Renaissance edition, 1908), which, like his various prefaces and essays, shows him to be a subtle literary critic.

As the new century dawned Davidson was hard at work on a series of 'Testaments', in which he gave definite expression to his philosophy and these were published over a seven year period; 'The Testament of a Vivisector' (1901), 'The Testament of a Man Forbid' (1901), 'The Testament of an Empire Builder' (1902), and 'The Testament of John Davidson' (1908).

Though he played down any thought of himself as a philosopher, he expounded an original philosophy which was at once materialistic and aristocratic.

His later verse, which is often fine rhetoric rather than poetry, expressed his belief which is summed up in the last words that he wrote, "Men are the universe become conscious; the simplest man should consider himself too great to be called after any name." Davidson professed to reject all existing philosophies, including that of Nietzsche, as inadequate. The poet planned to expand and expound on his revolutionary creed in a trilogy entitled 'God and Mammon'. Only two plays, however, were written, 'The Triumph of Mammon' (1907) and 'Mammon and his Message' (1908).

In addition to his own work Davidson was a noted translator of other works which included Montesquieu's 'Lettres Persanes' (1892), François Coppée's 'Pour la Couronne' in 1896 and Victor Hugo's 'Ruy Blas' in 1904, the former being produced as, 'For the Crown', at the Lyceum Theatre in 1896, the latter as 'A Queen's Romance' at the Imperial Theatre.

Frank Harris, a member of the Rhymers' Club and himself a writer of erotic literature described him in 1889 as: "... a little below middle height, but strongly built with square shoulders and remarkably fine face and head; the features were almost classically regular, the eyes dark brown and large, the forehead high, the hair and moustache black. His manners were perfectly frank and natural; he met everyone in the same unaffected kindly human way; I never saw a trace in him of snobbishness or incivility. Possibly a great man, I said to myself, certainly a man of genius, for simplicity of manner alone is in England almost a proof of extraordinary endowment."

In 1906 he was awarded a civil list pension of £100 per annum and George Bernard Shaw did what he could to help him financially. However other issues were also circling besides poverty. Ill-health, and his declining intellectual powers, amplified by the onset of cancer, caused profound hopelessness and clinical depression.

Late in 1908, Davidson left London to live in Penzance in Cornwall. On 23rd March 1909, he left his house and was not seen again. There seemed no sound reason not to believe that he had done so with the intention of drowning himself. On an examination of his office a new manuscript was found. It was a poetry book; 'Fleet Street Poems', with a letter bleakly stating confirming, "This will be my last book."

Indeed in his philosophic book 'The Testament of John Davidson', published the year before his death, he anticipates this fate:

"None should outlive his power. . . . Who kills
Himself subdues the conqueror of kings;
Exempt from death is he who takes his life;
My time has come."

Davidson's body was not discovered until 18th September in Mount's cave by some fishermen. In accordance with his will it was now buried at sea. Strangely it seemed Davidson's wish that none of his unpublished works, nor any biography be published and "no word except of my writing is ever to appear in any book of mine as long as the copyright endures."

Davidson's poetry was a key early influence on important Modernist poets, in particular, his compatriot Hugh MacDiarmid, Wallace Stevens and T.S. Eliot.

John Davidson – A Concise Bibliography

The North Wall (1885)
Diabolus Amans (1885) Verse drama
Bruce (1886) A drama in five acts
Smith (1888) A tragedy
An Unhistorical Pastoral, A Romantic Farce (1889)
Scaramouch in Naxos (1889)
Perfervid: The Career of Ninian Jamieson (1890) with 23 Original Illustrations by Harry Furniss
The Great Men, And a Practical Novelist (1891) Illustrated by E. J. Ellis.
In a Music Hall, and other Poems (1891)
Laura Ruthven's Widowhood (with C. J. Wills) (1892)
Fleet Street Eclogues (1893)
The Knight of the Maypole, (1903)
Sentences and Paragraphs (1893)
Ballads and Songs (1894)
Baptist Lake (1894)
A Random Itinerary (1894)
A Full and True Account of the Wonderful Mission of Earl Lavender (1895)
St. George's Day (1895)
Fleet Street Eclogues (Second Series) (1896)
Miss Armstrong's and Other Circumstances (1896)
The Pilgrimage of Strongsoul and Other Stories (1896)
New Ballads (1897)
Godfrida, a play (1898)
The Last Ballad (1899)
Self's the Man, A tragi-comedy (1901)
The Testament of a Man Forbid (1901)
The Testament of a Vivisector (1901)
The Testament of an Empire Builder (1902)
A Rosary (1903)
The Knight of the Maypole: A Comedy in Four Acts (1903)
The Testament of a Prime Minister (1904)
The Ballad of a Nun (1905)
The Theatrocrat: A Tragic Play of Church and State (1905)
Holiday and other poems, with a note on poetry (1906)
The Triumph of Mammon (1907)

Mammon and His Message (1908)
The Testament of John Davidson (1908)
Fleet Street and other Poems (1909)

He was also a contributor to 'The Yellow Book' periodical

As Translator

Montesquieu's Lettres Persanes (Persian Letters) (1892)
François Coppée's Pour la couronne (For the Crown) (1896)
Victor Hugo's Ruy Blas (A Queen's Romance) (1904)